FAIL FORWARD
90-DAY PROJECT PLANNER
2022

Fail Forward

90-DAY PROJECT PLANNER 2022

SUCCEED — IMPERFECTLY — WITH 4 BIG ANNUAL GOALS

JENNIFER NEWCOMB

To Nina Pearl and all the big dreamers of the world.

© 2021 Jennifer Newcomb

All rights reserved.

Published by Spring Press.

This book or parts thereof may not be reproduced in any form, stored in any retrieval system, or transmitted in any form by any means—electronic, mechanical, photocopy, recording, or otherwise—without prior written permission of the publisher, except as provided by United States of America copyright law. For permission requests, write to the author, at "Jen@LetsFailForward.com".

ISBN: 978-0-578-32808-9

Squirrel Pilot cover illustration © Christy Freeman /christystudios.com

Come say hi at jennifernewcomb.com

Is this you and your project?

- You're tired of cycling through attack and escape modes.

- You keep trying new planners and apps, but it doesn't help.

- You don't want the guilt and erratic progress to trip you up anymore — you want to actually achieve your important goal.

Try this instead!

- Stay inspired and optimistic, know what to work on and steadily move forward until you finish.

- Failing forward is based on two central ideas from the book, The Path of Least Resistance" by Robert Fritz:
    - challenges and failures are good and necessary
    - weirdly, the *gap* between what you want and what you have contains all the power!

- Learn from a bestselling author on collaboration and creativity who's taken big risks that flopped (bankruptcy, dead-end projects that took years), but always recovers with this system.

How to do it:

1. scan the big picture (5 mins.)
2. jump in with the quick start guide (10 mins.)
3. flip back to the tips if you get stuck (whenever)

PHOTO BY HANS VETH

TABLE OF CONTENTS

1
PLAN FOR PROCRASTINATION
The big picture
1

2
THE MESSY TRUTH CREATES MOMENTUM
A quick start guide
5

3
PLANNER
Your experiment awaits
9

4
RESOLVE MYSTERIOUS SETBACKS
Troubleshooting tips
281

5
RESOURCES
Recommended books and staying in touch
289

EXPANDED CONTENTS

1. PLAN FOR PROCRASTINATION
The big picture — 1
- How traditional planners set you up to fail — 2
- Your superpower: honesty + missed goals — 3
- Stop stockpiling guilt and make fresh starts — 4

2. THE MESSY TRUTH CREATES MOMENTUM
A quick start guide — 5
- The secret to failing forward: creative tension — 6
- Outwit perfection and pretend progress — 7
- 3 questions to generate energy — 8

3. PLANNER
Your experiment awaits — 9
- Capture a meaningful goal — 14
- Identify strengths and avoidance — 16
- Check in and remember resources — 18
- Transform dread into actionable tasks — 20
- Fuel creative tension with wins and losses — 23

4. RESOLVE MYSTERIOUS SETBACKS
Troubleshooting tips — 273
- Motivate: remove self-sabotage — 276
- Calm: diffuse escapism — 277
- Act: get back on track when you drift — 278
- Grow: find childlike lessons for hard tasks — 279
- Energize: build confidence with brave honesty — 280

5. RESOURCES
Recommended books and staying in touch — 281

PHOTO BY JESSE LITTLE

01

Plan for Procrastination
The big picture

How traditional planners set you up to fail

Try failing forward instead!

Your superpower: honesty + missed goals

We all consistently fall short of our plans and get stuck.
Unfortunately, most planners provide a rigid template for success, not reality.

Every important goal involves fear, confusion and resistance.
Procrastinating, avoiding and being overwhelmed is normal.

Messing up too many to-dos makes us feel stressed, guilty and inadequate.
That means most of us are tempted to fudge progress in our planners.

The simple system for failing forward

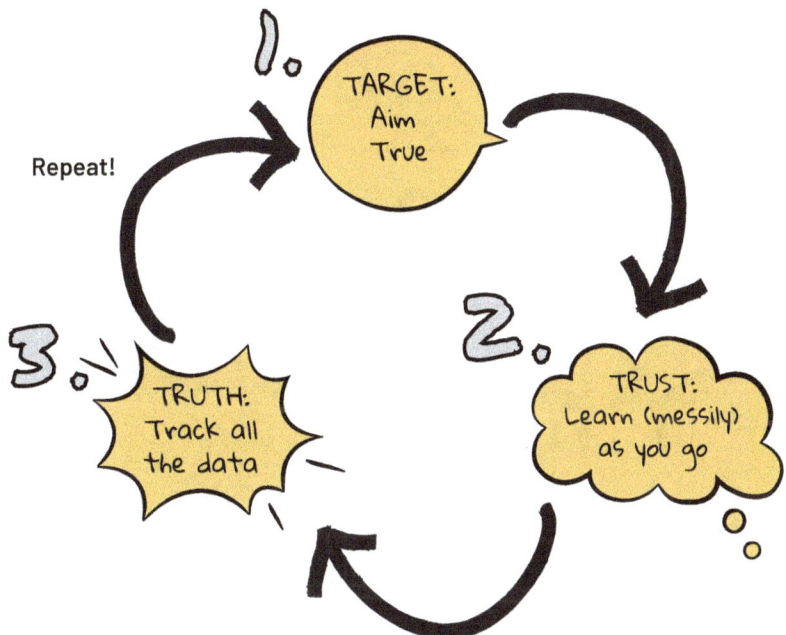

> **Ironically, your superpower for reaching your goals is very simple: tell the truth.**

Don't lie to yourself about stalling, getting lost and missing deadlines.
It's uncomfortable, but honesty creates an endless fuel to power you forward.

Truth builds trust and helps you keep learning and take imperfect action.
You'll get back on track with less stress and figure out what to do.

No need for some flawless upward trajectory.
Just embrace the chaotic nature of real life!

Stop stockpiling guilt and make fresh starts

How the five Fail Forward worksheets build upon each other.

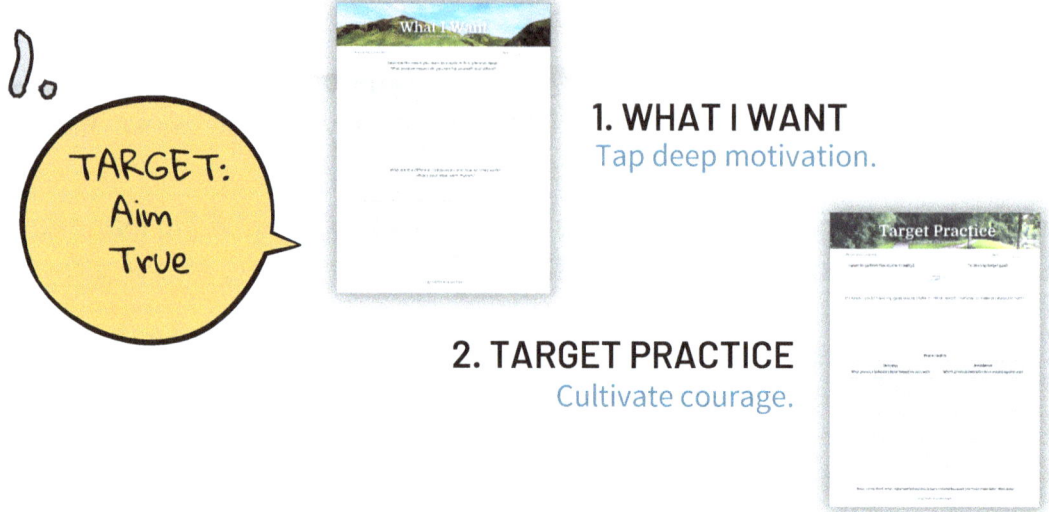

1.

TARGET: Aim True

1. WHAT I WANT
Tap deep motivation.

2. TARGET PRACTICE
Cultivate courage.

2.

TRUST: Learn (messily) as you go

3. CURRENT REALITY
Manage fear. Remember resources.

4. MICRO-TARGETS
Create best guess to-dos.

3.

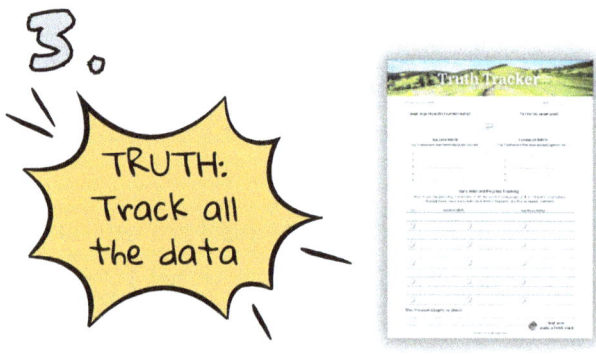

TRUTH: Track all the data

5. TRUTH TRACKER
Report real progress, then reset!

You'll also keep the best pages from traditional planners.

PHOTO BY ANDREY SVISTUNOV

02

The messy truth creates momentum

A quick start guide

The secret to failing forward: creative tension

Mind the gap

Wanting to reach a goal is uncomfortable.

You want it, but don't have it. It's going to take a lot of work to get there. Maybe you've even failed at it before.

You're simultaneously straddling two very different states:

where you are right now

and

where you want to be

The gap between those two states creates tension, like a twisted rubber band.

That creative tension wants to resolve itself.

Feeling this gap, this discomfort is actually a good thing.

You're going to harness that trapped energy to help you reach your goal — not wish it away.

You just need to learn how!

Outwit perfection and pretend progress

We typically try one of three ways to reach our goal: overpower, avoid or create.

Overpower
We keep our focus on how amazing it will be when we finally succeed, ignoring current reality and the scope of the tasks needed to get from A to B. We frame our situation as better than it is to stay pumped up and motivated.

Our high-intensity efforts aren't sustainable and we eventually run out of steam.

Avoid
We use deadlines and the threat of negative consequences to prompt action, so our behavior is really more about trying to avert scenarios we fear — not achieving our goal. This makes us see the situation as worse than it really is. It also makes us eventually want to escape our project altogether.

When we give up, we're relieved.

PHOTO: ERIK MCLEAN

PHOTO: JEHYUN SUNG

Create
We regularly assess how it's really going without fear or shame. We hold any unpleasant facts about the present AND our goal in mind at the same time to generate creative tension. We know that doing this will help propel us forward.

Confusion, stumbles, failure — it's all fodder that you'll use (and expect to have) on your journey.

3 questions to generate energy

As you experiment, keep asking yourself:

What do I want?
Where do things stand now?
What actions do I need to take
to create what I want?

Taking action, you'll see that:

It works. It doesn't work. It works. It kind of works. Etc.

So then what?

Failure = Neutral Facts

Use the truth about your progress, both good and bad, to generate creative tension and make better decisions in imperfect pursuit of your goal.

A scientist doesn't conduct an experiment, then throw out all the data if she doesn't get the result she was expecting. Your failures provide valuable information about what works and what doesn't.

When you only track successes, you only have half the data. That means you're even less likely to succeed next time!

Ready? Let's go!

Now it's your turn. Flip the page to get started. Keep in mind:

- Make a mess. No perfection allowed!
- Paperclip or fold back important pages.
- Fill out journal pages when the time is right.
- Follow the squirrel examples provided for new pages and see the tips in the back if you need help.

PHOTO BY ALEX LAUZON

03
Planner

Your experiment awaits!

The fail forward workflow

Use the 5 fail forward worksheets with 5 traditional planner pages.

But don't worry! The regular planner pages are self-explanatory. You'll learn how to fill out the worksheets right before you use them.

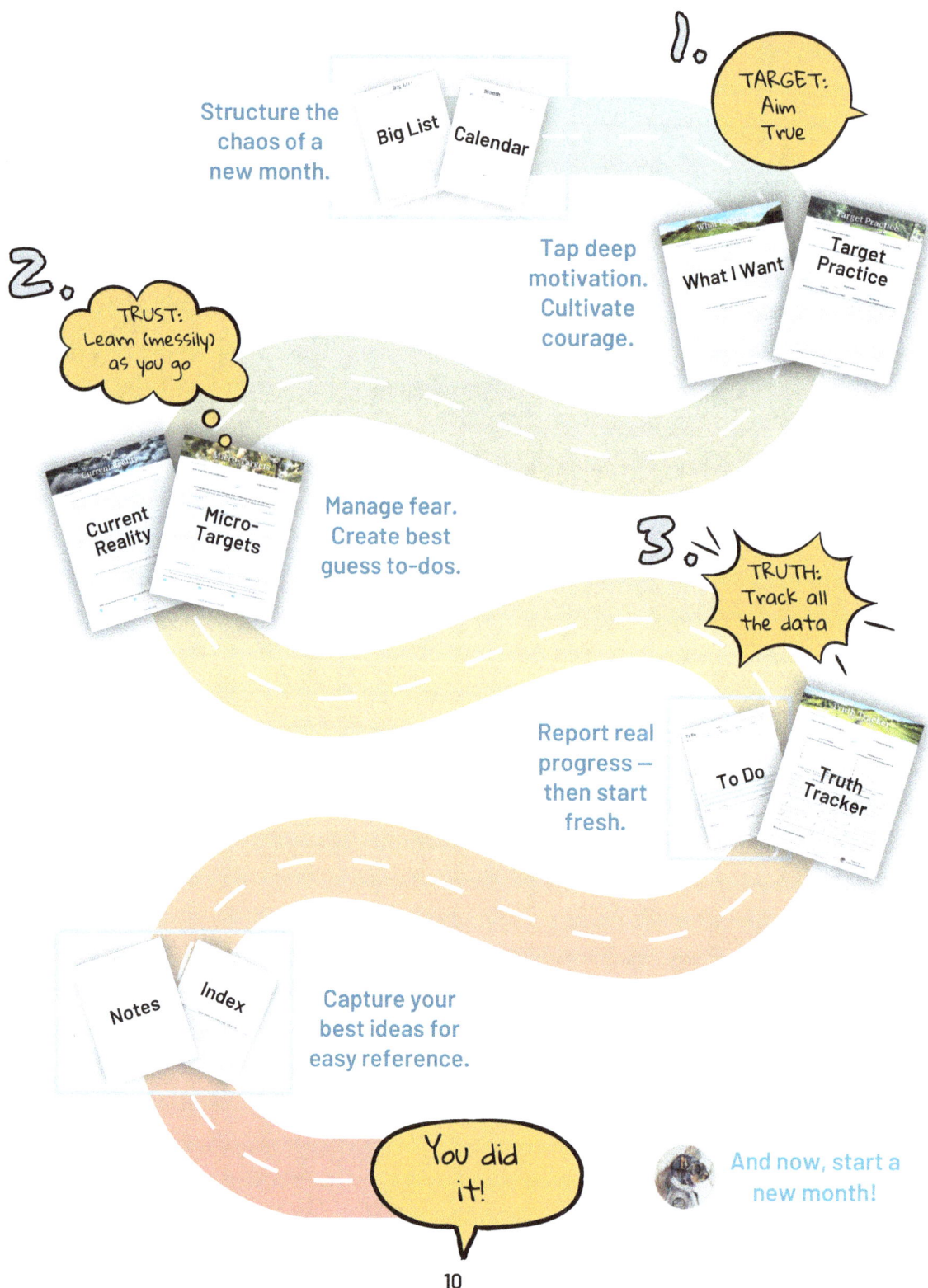

Q1 January

PHOTO BY ZHAN ZHANG

"In the world, everything is connected, and no one is an island."
- Ken Mogi, The Little Book of Ikigai

What do I want to remember this month about making a fresh start, taking risks and the power of imperfection?

January Big List

Get the to-dos of your life out of your mind and onto the page. (Not in order!)

Draw new category boxes as needed. Sample categories: Health, Family, Work, Finances, Household, School, Etc.
Also: Projects, Weird Hassles, Power Hour, Fun, Friends, Pets, Decluttering, Misc.

structure the chaos

Q1 - January

Sunday	Monday	Tuesday	Wednesday	Thursday	Friday	Saturday
26	27	28	29	30	31	1
2	3	4	5	6	7	8
9	10	11	12	13	14	15
16	17	18	19	20	21	22
23	24	25	26	27	28	29
30	31	1	2	3	4	5

Notes

structure the chaos

 # Capture a meaningful goal
Tap deep motivation.

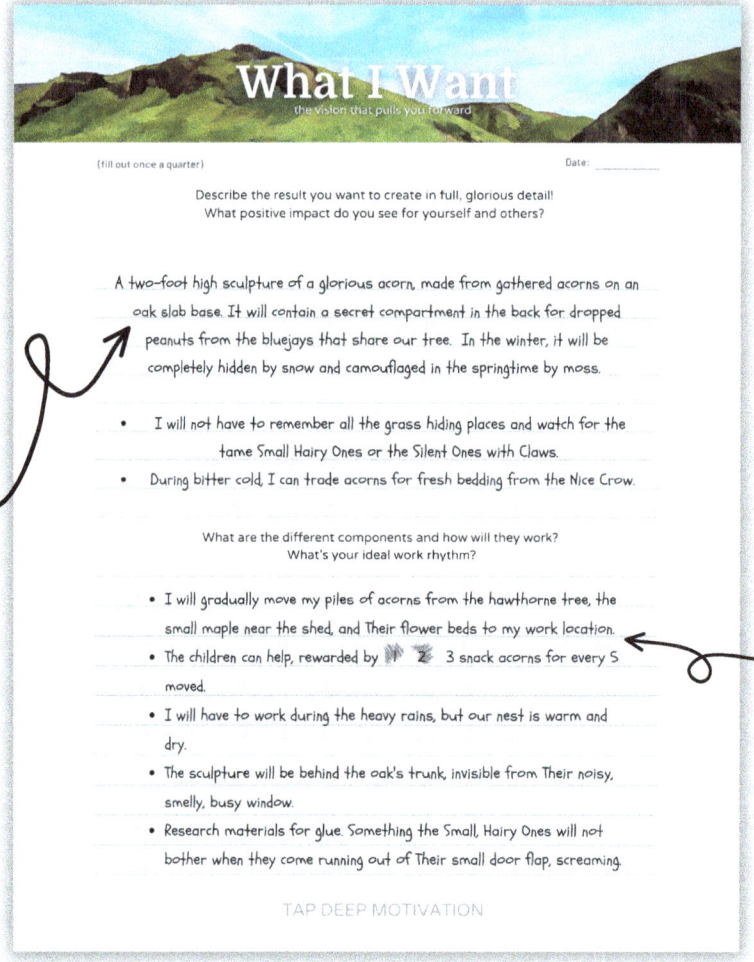

Feel your way into happiness

Make it vivid and real. Don't worry about how it's going to happen or whether it will. Just get the dream down.

What are you longing to create?

Allow it to be imperfect and incomplete.

This is just a first pass. You'll have plenty of chances to fine-tune things later.

What phrases and bullet points can you quickly write down?

Move away from the long shadows

Competing against others can be invigorating! But it can also compromise your goal.

In carving out your own path, what outcome would bring YOU the most joy?

What I Want
the vision that pulls you forward

(fill out once a quarter)   Date: _____

Describe the result you want to create in full, glorious detail!
What positive impact do you see for yourself and others?

What are the different components and how will they work? What's your ideal work rhythm? What are 1 or 2 short-term or intermediate milestones?

tap deep motivation

TARGET: Aim True

Identify strengths and avoidance habits
Cultivate courage.

Your starting point. → (on worksheet)

Your goal. → (on worksheet)

Check for hidden sabotage.
Imagine your success was assured. Describe any unwanted demands you assume you'll have to accept.

What would you prefer instead?

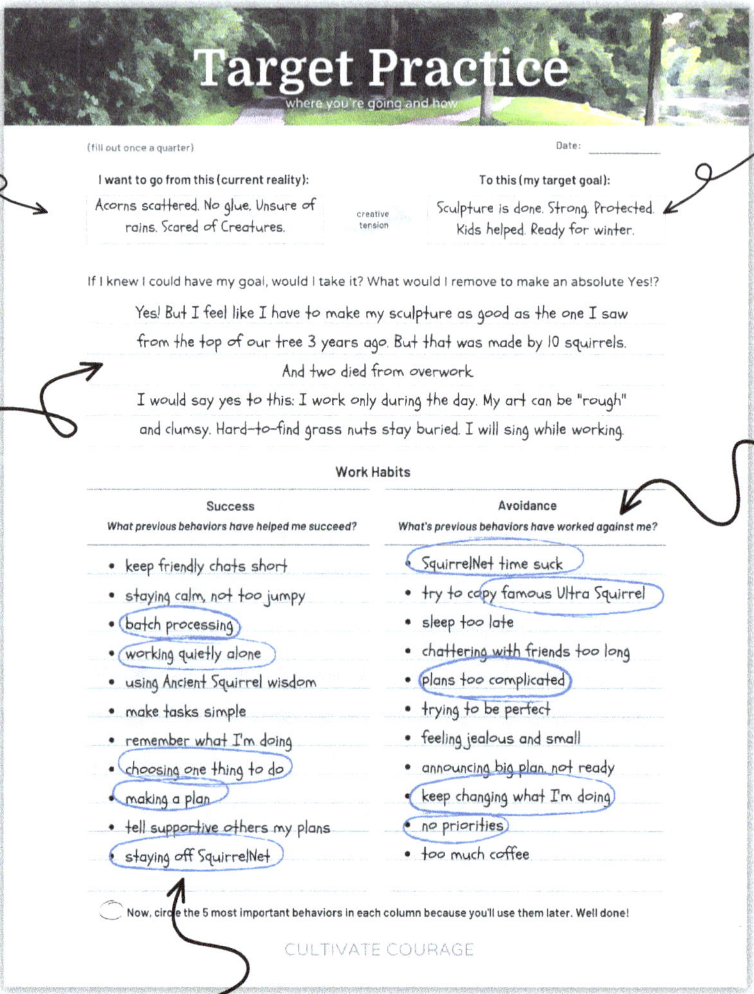

Name your escapist habits.
We all have them: our favorite, but unhelpful ways to cope with thorny problems and unpleasant tasks.

What behaviors have worked against you before?

Make your success traits visible.
These are the reliable skills and habits you feel good about. You probably take them for granted!

What behaviors have worked to create success before?

Target Practice
where you're going and how

(fill out once a quarter)   Date: _____

I want to go from this (current reality):
Acorns scattered. No glue. Unsure of rains. Scared of Creatures.

creative tension

To this (my target goal):
Sculpture is done. Strong. Protected. Kids helped. Ready for winter.

If I knew I could have my goal, would I take it? What would I remove to make an absolute Yes!?

Yes! But I feel like I have to make my sculpture as good as the one I saw from the top of our tree 3 years ago. But that was made by 10 squirrels. And two died from overwork.

I would say yes to this: I work only during the day. My art can be "rough" and clumsy. Hard-to-find grass nuts stay buried. I will sing while working.

Work Habits

Success — What previous behaviors have helped me succeed?	Avoidance — What's previous behaviors have worked against me?
• keep friendly chats short	• (SquirrelNet time suck)
• staying calm, not too jumpy	• (try to copy famous Ultra Squirrel)
• (batch processing)	• sleep too late
• (working quietly alone)	• chattering with friends too long
• using Ancient Squirrel wisdom	• (plans too complicated)
• make tasks simple	• trying to be perfect
• remember what I'm doing	• feeling jealous and small
• (choosing one thing to do)	• announcing big plan, not ready
• (making a plan)	• (keep changing what I'm doing)
• tell supportive others my plans	• (no priorities)
• (staying off SquirrelNet)	• too much coffee

Now, circle the 5 most important behaviors in each column because you'll use them later. Well done!

CULTIVATE COURAGE

16

Target Practice
where you're going and how

(fill out once a quarter)   Date: _____

I want to go from this (current reality):   **To this (my target goal):**

creative tension

If I knew I could have my goal, would I take it? What would I remove to make an absolute Yes!?

_____

_____

_____

_____

Work Habits

Success	**Avoidance**
What previous behaviors have helped me succeed?	What previous behaviors have worked against me?

Now, circle the 5 most important behaviors in each column because you'll use them later. Well done!

cultivate courage

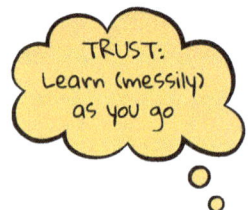

Check in and remember resources

Manage fear.

Lessen anxiety by catching it

Jot it all down, the good and the bad. No one will see this but you.

What's going well? What's confusing?

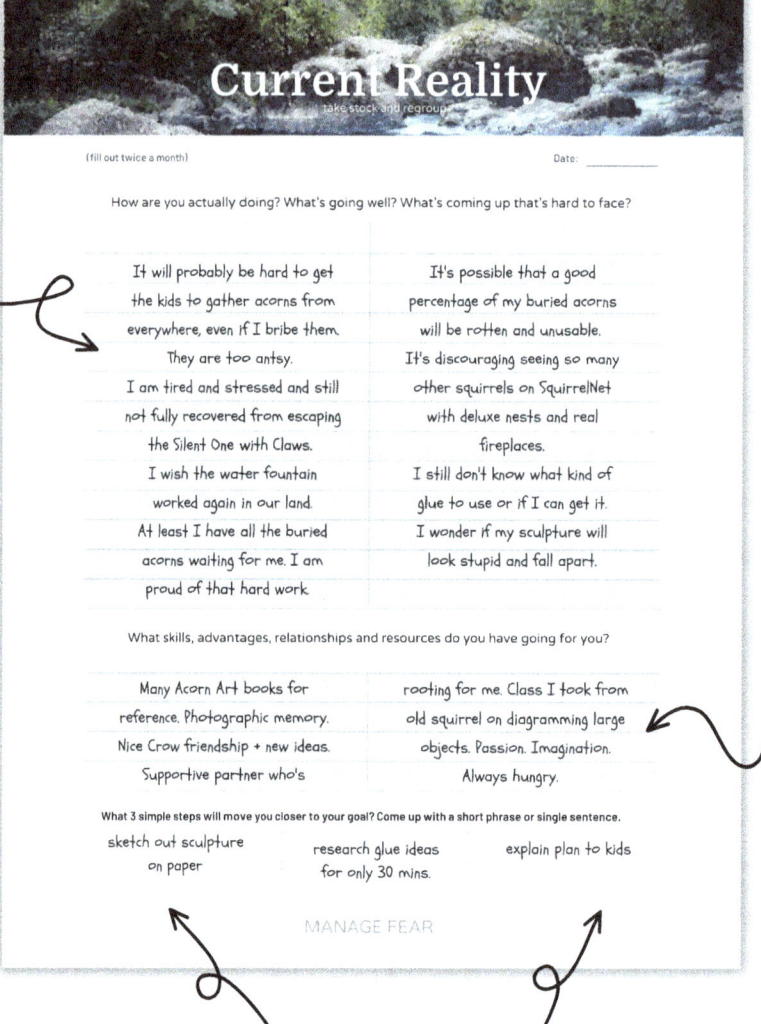

Reflect back with kindness

A genuine friend reminds you of all you've got going for you when you're struggling. Be that person for yourself.

What skills and knowledge do you already have?

Make your 3 best guesses from a hat

Brainstorm the natural next steps on your journey. No perfection required!

If a good friend with the same goal asked for your advice, what would you tell them to do?

Current Reality
take stock and regroup

(fill out twice a month)   Date: _____

How are you actually doing? What's going well? What's coming up that's hard to face?

What skills, advantages, relationships and resources do you have going for you?

What 3 simple steps will move you closer to your goal? Come up with a short phrase or single sentence.

manage fear

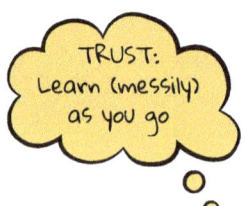

TRUST: Learn (messily) as you go

Transform dread into actionable tasks

Create best guess to-dos.

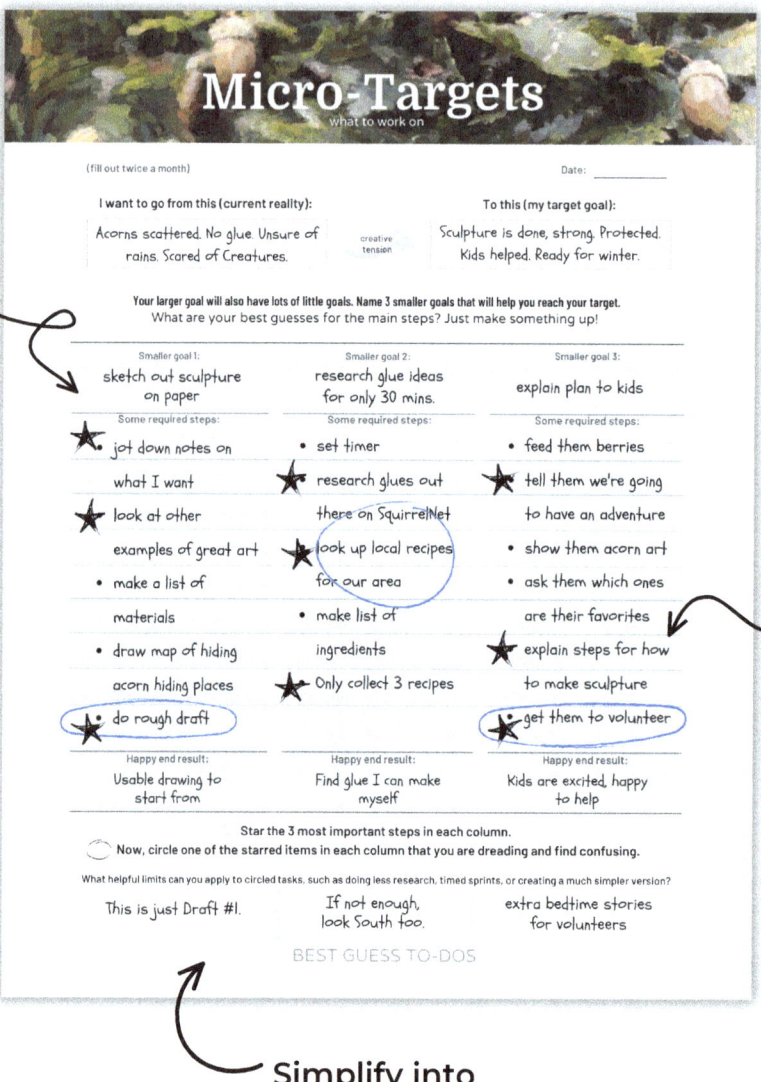

Copy your 3 smaller steps here

Transfer your best guesses for what to do from Current Reality.

What's a positive outcome that would make you happy?

Overcome paralysis by winging it

It doesn't matter if your knowledge is incomplete here. You can still imagine the beginnings of a loose plan and change it later.

How would you tell a smart child how to get from A-to-B?

Simplify into laughably small steps

After circling your most feared tasks above, shrink them down to make them even more doable.

What's one short phrase per to-do task?

Micro-Targets
what to work on

(fill out twice a month)   Date: _____

I want to go from this (current reality):   **To this (my target goal):**

[   ]   creative tension →   [   ]

Your larger goal will also have lots of little goals. Name 3 smaller goals that will help you reach your target.
What are your best guesses for the main steps? Just make something up!

Smaller goal 1:	Smaller goal 2:	Smaller goal 3:
Some required steps:	Some required steps:	Some required steps:
Happy end result:	Happy end result:	Happy end result:

For each column: Star the 3 most important steps. Then circle the hardest, most confusing starred item.

What helpful limits can you apply to circled tasks, such as less research, timed sprints, or creating a simpler version?

create best guess to-dos

Almost there!

Last worksheet instructions.

This placeholder has been added for January only

so that all the proper pages face each other.

Fuel creative tension with wins and losses

Report real progress — then reset.

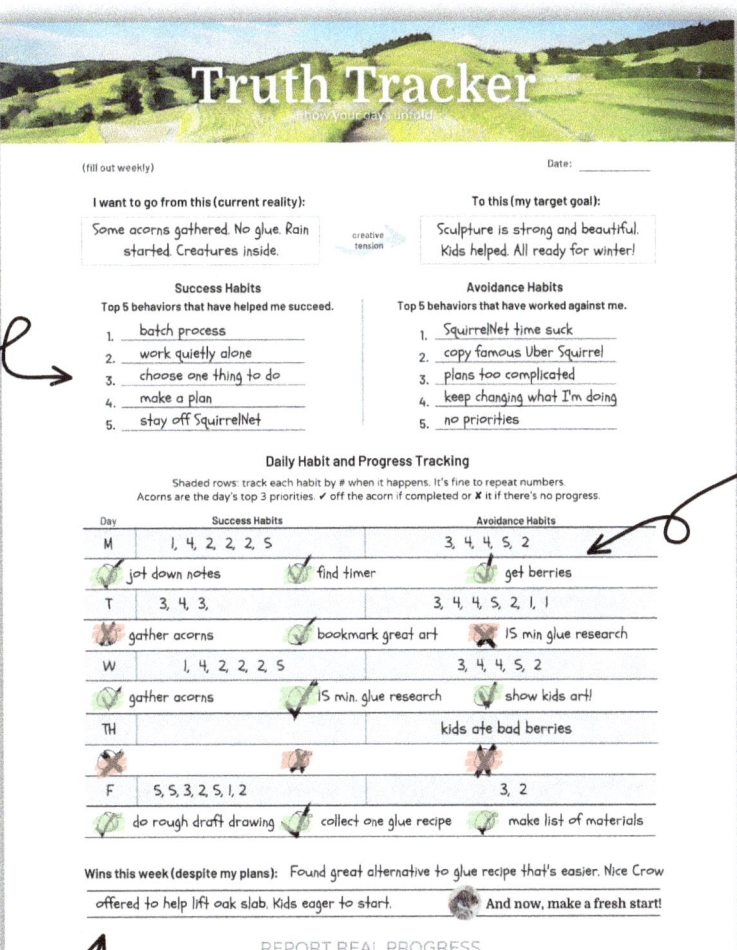

Turn your work habits into power tools

Copy your circled success and avoidance behaviors from Target Practice here so you can catch them in action.

What are your most fruitful and cringeworthy work habits?

Track all data as it happens

Choose from earlier best guesses for your daily priorities. Note your good and bad habits in progress — no guilt or blame allowed.

Can you log data like a curious, impartial scientist?

It was what it was, now reset with optimism

Highlight your imperfect progress with colors! Instead of an open loop of guilt and blame, focus on what you did well this week in the face of personal and life challenges.

What can you be proud of, big or small?

23

To Do

To generate momentum, scan What I Want and Micro-Targets.

	Monday - 3	Tuesday - 4	Wednesday - 5	Thursday - 6	Friday - 7
Appts/Errands					
Tasks (circle top 3)					
Focus Blocks					

Saturday - 8	Sunday - 9	Must Do This Week / Notes

Truth Tracker

how your days unfold

(fill out weekly)   Date: _____

I want to go from this (current reality):   **To this (my target goal):**

creative tension →

Success Habits
1. _____
2. _____
3. _____
4. _____
5. _____

Avoidance Habits
1. _____
2. _____
3. _____
4. _____
5. _____

Daily Progress

Acorns: top 3 daily priorities. ✔ if completed or ✘ if unfinished.
Shaded rows: track each habit by # whenever it happens.

Day

Top 3 Habits

Weekend

Wins this week (despite plans):

report real progress

And now, make a fresh start!

To Do

To generate momentum,
scan What I Want and Micro-Targets.

	Monday - 10	Tuesday - 11	Wednesday - 12	Thursday - 13	Friday - 14
Appts/Errands					
Tasks (circle top 3)					
Focus Blocks					

Saturday - 15	Sunday - 16	Must Do This Week / Notes

Truth Tracker
how your days unfold

(fill out weekly) Date: _____

I want to go from this (current reality):

[   ]

creative tension

To this (my target goal):

[   ]

Success Habits
1. _____
2. _____
3. _____
4. _____
5. _____

Avoidance Habits
1. _____
2. _____
3. _____
4. _____
5. _____

Daily Progress

Acorns: top 3 daily priorities. ✓ if completed or ✗ if unfinished.
Shaded rows: track each habit by # whenever it happens.

Day

Top 3 Habits

Weekend

Wins this week (despite plans):

_____

_____

report real progress

And now, make a fresh start!

Current Reality
take stock and regroup

(fill out twice a month)　　　　　　　　　　　　　　　　　　　　　　Date: _____

How are you actually doing? What's going well? What's coming up that's hard to face?

What skills, advantages, relationships and resources do you have going for you?

What 3 simple steps will move you closer to your goal? Come up with a short phrase or single sentence.

manage fear

Micro-Targets
what to work on

(fill out twice a month)　　　　　　　　　　　　　　　　　　　　Date: _____

I want to go from this (current reality):　　　　　　　　**To this (my target goal):**

[　　　　　　　　　　　]　　*creative tension* →　　[　　　　　　　　　　　]

Your larger goal will also have lots of little goals. Name 3 smaller goals that will help you reach your target.
What are your best guesses for the main steps? Just make something up!

Smaller goal 1:	Smaller goal 2:	Smaller goal 3:
Some required steps:	Some required steps:	Some required steps:
Happy end result:	Happy end result:	Happy end result:

For each column: Star the 3 most important steps. Then circle the hardest, most confusing starred item.

What helpful limits can you apply to circled tasks, such as less research, timed sprints, or creating a simpler version?

create best guess to-dos

To Do

To generate momentum,
scan What I Want and Micro-Targets.

	Monday - 17	Tuesday - 18	Wednesday - 19	Thursday - 20	Friday - 21
Appts/Errands					
Tasks (circle top 3)					
Focus Blocks					

Saturday - 22	Sunday - 23	Must Do This Week / Notes

Truth Tracker
how your days unfold

(fill out weekly) Date: _____

I want to go from this (current reality): → creative tension → **To this (my target goal):**

Success Habits:
1. _____
2. _____
3. _____
4. _____
5. _____

Avoidance Habits:
1. _____
2. _____
3. _____
4. _____
5. _____

Daily Progress

Acorns: top 3 daily priorities. ✓ if completed or ✗ if unfinished.
Shaded rows: track each habit by # whenever it happens.

Day | Top 3 Habits | Weekend

Wins this week (despite plans):
_____

_____

And now, make a fresh start!

report real progress

To Do

To generate momentum,
scan What I Want and Micro-Targets.

	Monday - 24	Tuesday - 25	Wednesday - 26	Thursday - 27	Friday - 28
Appts/Errands					
Tasks (circle top 3)					
Focus Blocks					

Saturday - 29	Sunday - 30	Must Do This Week / Notes

Truth Tracker
how your days unfold

(fill out weekly)   Date: _____

I want to go from this (current reality):   **To this (my target goal):**

[   ]   *creative tension*   [   ]

Success Habits
1. _____
2. _____
3. _____
4. _____
5. _____

Avoidance Habits
1. _____
2. _____
3. _____
4. _____
5. _____

Daily Progress

Acorns: top 3 daily priorities. ✓ if completed or ✗ if unfinished.
Shaded rows: track each habit by # whenever it happens.

Day

Top 3 Habits

Weekend

Wins this week (despite plans):

_____

_____

report real progress

And now, make a fresh start!

NOTES
Use this space to do extra check-ins and brainstorm micro-targets, along with new ideas.

capture your best ideas

NOTES

capture your best ideas

NOTES

capture your best ideas

NOTES

capture your best ideas

NOTES

PAGE #   INDEX: IMPORTANT NOTES FROM THIS MONTH

capture your best ideas

Q1 - February

PHOTO BY SARAH WOLFE

"Be especially careful not to confuse effort with result or you will end up with a system that is producing effort, not result."
- Donella H. Meadows, Thinking in Systems

What do I want to remember this month about making a fresh start, taking risks and the power of imperfection?

February Big List

Get the to-dos of your life out of your mind and onto the page. (Not in order!)

Draw new category boxes as needed. Sample categories: Health, Family, Work, Finances, Household, School, Etc.
Also: Projects, Weird Hassles, Power Hour, Fun, Friends, Pets, Decluttering, Misc.

structure the chaos

Q1 - FEBRUARY

Sunday	Monday	Tuesday	Wednesday	Thursday	Friday	Saturday
30	31	1	2	3	4	5
6	7	8	9	10	11	12
13	14	15	16	17	18	19
20	21	22	23	24	25	26
27	28	1	2	3	4	5
6	7	8	9	10	11	12

Notes

structure the chaos

Current Reality
take stock and regroup

(fill out twice a month) Date: _____

Has your big goal changed? What's going well? What's coming up that's hard to face?

_____
_____
_____
_____
_____
_____
_____
_____
_____
_____
_____
_____

What skills, advantages, relationships and resources do you have going for you?

_____
_____
_____

What 3 simple steps will move you closer to your goal? Come up with a short phrase or single sentence.

manage fear

Micro-Targets
what to work on

(fill out twice a month) Date: _____

I want to go from this (current reality): **To this (my target goal):**

[ ] *creative tension* → [ ]

Your larger goal will also have lots of little goals. Name 3 smaller goals that will help you reach your target.
What are your best guesses for the main steps? Just make something up!

Smaller goal 1:	Smaller goal 2:	Smaller goal 3:
Some required steps:	Some required steps:	Some required steps:
Happy end result:	Happy end result:	Happy end result:

For each column: Star the 3 most important steps. Then circle the hardest, most confusing starred item.

What helpful limits can you apply to circled tasks, such as less research, timed sprints, or creating a simpler version?

create best guess to-dos

43

To Do

To generate momentum, scan What I Want and Micro-Targets.

	Monday - 31	Tuesday - 1	Wednesday - 2	Thursday - 3	Friday - 4
Appts/Errands					
Tasks (circle top 3)					
Focus Blocks					

Saturday - 5	Sunday - 6	Must Do This Week / Notes

Truth Tracker
how your days unfold

(fill out weekly)   Date: _____

I want to go from this (current reality):   *creative tension*   **To this (my target goal):**

Success Habits
1. _____
2. _____
3. _____
4. _____
5. _____

Avoidance Habits
1. _____
2. _____
3. _____
4. _____
5. _____

Daily Progress

Acorns: top 3 daily priorities. ✔ if completed or ✘ if unfinished.
Shaded rows: track each habit by # whenever it happens.

Day

Top 3 Habits

Weekend

Wins this week (despite plans):

_____

And now, make a fresh start!

report real progress

To Do

To generate momentum, scan What I Want and Micro-Targets.

	Monday - 7	Tuesday - 8	Wednesday - 9	Thursday - 10	Friday - 11
Appts/Errands					
Tasks (circle top 3)					
Focus Blocks					

Saturday - 12	Sunday - 13	Must Do This Week / Notes

Truth Tracker
how your days unfold

(fill out weekly)   Date: _____

I want to go from this (current reality):   **To this (my target goal):**

[   ]   *creative tension* →   [   ]

Success Habits
1. _____
2. _____
3. _____
4. _____
5. _____

Avoidance Habits
1. _____
2. _____
3. _____
4. _____
5. _____

Daily Progress

Acorns: top 3 daily priorities. ✓ if completed or ✗ if unfinished.
Shaded rows: track each habit by # whenever it happens.

Day / Top 3 Habits / Weekend

Wins this week (despite plans):
_____

report real progress

And now, make a fresh start!

Current Reality
take stock and regroup

(fill out twice a month) Date: _____

How are you actually doing? What's going well? What's coming up that's hard to face?

What skills, advantages, relationships and resources do you have going for you?

What 3 simple steps will move you closer to your goal? Come up with a short phrase or single sentence.

manage fear

Micro-Targets
what to work on

(fill out twice a month) Date: _____

I want to go from this (current reality):   **To this (my target goal):**

[   ]   *creative tension*   [   ]

Your larger goal will also have lots of little goals. Name 3 smaller goals that will help you reach your target.
What are your best guesses for the main steps? Just make something up!

Smaller goal 1:	Smaller goal 2:	Smaller goal 3:
Some required steps:	Some required steps:	Some required steps:
Happy end result:	Happy end result:	Happy end result:

For each column: Star the 3 most important steps. Then circle the hardest, most confusing starred item.

What helpful limits can you apply to circled tasks, such as less research, timed sprints, or creating a simpler version?

create best guess to-dos

To Do

To generate momentum, scan What I Want and Micro-Targets.

	Monday - 14	Tuesday - 15	Wednesday - 16	Thursday - 17	Friday - 18
Appts/Errands					
Tasks (circle top 3)					
Focus Blocks					

Saturday - 19	Sunday - 20	Must Do This Week / Notes

Truth Tracker
how your days unfold

(fill out weekly)   Date: _____

I want to go from this (current reality):   **To this (my target goal):**

[   ]   *creative tension*   [   ]

Success Habits
1. _____
2. _____
3. _____
4. _____
5. _____

Avoidance Habits
1. _____
2. _____
3. _____
4. _____
5. _____

Daily Progress

Acorns: top 3 daily priorities. ✔ if completed or ✘ if unfinished.
Shaded rows: track each habit by # whenever it happens.

Day

Top 3 Habits

Weekend

Wins this week (despite plans):

_____

_____

report real progress

And now, make a fresh start!

To Do

To generate momentum,
scan What I Want and Micro-Targets.

	Monday - 21	Tuesday - 22	Wednesday - 23	Thursday - 24	Friday - 25
Appts/Errands					
Tasks (circle top 3)					
Focus Blocks					

Saturday - 26	Sunday - 27	Must Do This Week / Notes

52

Truth Tracker
how your days unfold

(fill out weekly) Date: _____

I want to go from this (current reality):

[_____]

creative tension →

To this (my target goal):

[_____]

Success Habits
1. _____
2. _____
3. _____
4. _____
5. _____

Avoidance Habits
1. _____
2. _____
3. _____
4. _____
5. _____

Daily Progress

Acorns: top 3 daily priorities. ✔ if completed or ✘ if unfinished.
Shaded rows: track each habit by # whenever it happens.

Day

Top 3 Habits

Weekend

Wins this week (despite plans):

_____

report real progress

And now, make a fresh start!

NOTES

Use this space to do extra check-ins and brainstorm micro-targets, along with new ideas.

capture your best ideas

NOTES

capture your best ideas

NOTES

capture your best ideas

NOTES

capture your best ideas

NOTES

PAGE #   INDEX: IMPORTANT NOTES FROM THIS MONTH

capture your best ideas

Q1 - March

PHOTO BY CATHY HOLEWINSKI

"...To figure out something new, your best bet is to turn off your precision-focused thinking and turn on your 'big picture' diffuse mode."
- Barbara Oakley, A Mind for Numbers

What do I want to remember this month about making a fresh start, taking risks and the power of imperfection?

March Big List

Get the to-dos of your life out of your mind and onto the page. (Not in order!)

Draw new category boxes as needed. Sample categories: Health, Family, Work, Finances, Household, School, Etc.
Also: Projects, Weird Hassles, Power Hour, Fun, Friends, Pets, Decluttering, Misc.

structure the chaos

Q1 - March

Sunday	Monday	Tuesday	Wednesday	Thursday	Friday	Saturday
27	28	1	2	3	4	5
6	7	8	9	10	11	12
13	14	15	16	17	18	19
20	21	22	23	24	25	26
27	28	29	30	31	1	2
3	4	5	6	7	8	9

Notes

structure the chaos

Current Reality
take stock and regroup

(fill out twice a month) Date: _____

Has your big goal changed? What's going well? What's coming up that's hard to face?

What skills, advantages, relationships and resources do you have going for you?

What 3 simple steps will move you closer to your goal? Come up with a short phrase or single sentence.

manage fear

Micro-Targets
what to work on

(fill out twice a month)   Date: _____

I want to go from this (current reality):   **To this (my target goal):**

[ ]   *creative tension* →   [ ]

Your larger goal will also have lots of little goals. Name 3 smaller goals that will help you reach your target.
What are your best guesses for the main steps? Just make something up!

Smaller goal 1:	Smaller goal 2:	Smaller goal 3:
Some required steps:	Some required steps:	Some required steps:
Happy end result:	Happy end result:	Happy end result:

For each column: Star the 3 most important steps. Then circle the hardest, most confusing starred item.

What helpful limits can you apply to circled tasks, such as less research, timed sprints, or creating a simpler version?

create best guess to-dos

To Do

To generate momentum, scan What I Want and Micro-Targets.

	Monday - 28	Tuesday - 1	Wednesday - 2	Thursday - 3	Friday - 4
Appts/Errands					
Tasks (circle top 3)					
Focus Blocks					

Saturday - 5	Sunday - 6	Must Do This Week / Notes

64

Truth Tracker

how your days unfold

(fill out weekly) Date: _____

I want to go from this (current reality):

[   ]

creative tension

To this (my target goal):

[   ]

Success Habits
1. _____
2. _____
3. _____
4. _____
5. _____

Avoidance Habits
1. _____
2. _____
3. _____
4. _____
5. _____

Daily Progress

Acorns: top 3 daily priorities. ✔ if completed or ✘ if unfinished.
Shaded rows: track each habit by # whenever it happens.

Day

Top 3 Habits

Weekend

Wins this week (despite plans):

_____

report real progress

And now, make a fresh start!

To Do

To generate momentum,
scan What I Want and Micro-Targets.

	Monday - 7	Tuesday - 8	Wednesday - 9	Thursday - 10	Friday - 11
Appts/Errands					
Tasks (circle top 3)					
Focus Blocks					

	Saturday - 12	Sunday - 13	Must Do This Week / Notes

66

Truth Tracker
how your days unfold

(fill out weekly) Date: _____

I want to go from this (current reality):

[   ]

creative tension

To this (my target goal):

[   ]

Success Habits:
1. _____
2. _____
3. _____
4. _____
5. _____

Avoidance Habits:
1. _____
2. _____
3. _____
4. _____
5. _____

Daily Progress

Acorns: top 3 daily priorities. ✓ if completed or ✗ if unfinished.
Shaded rows: track each habit by # whenever it happens.

Day / Top 3 Habits / Weekend

Wins this week (despite plans):

_____

report real progress

And now, make a fresh start!

Current Reality
take stock and regroup

(fill out twice a month) Date: _____

How are you actually doing? What's going well? What's coming up that's hard to face?

What skills, advantages, relationships and resources do you have going for you?

What 3 simple steps will move you closer to your goal? Come up with a short phrase or single sentence.

manage fear

Micro-Targets
what to work on

(fill out twice a month)   Date: _____

I want to go from this (current reality):   **To this (my target goal):**

creative tension

Your larger goal will also have lots of little goals. Name 3 smaller goals that will help you reach your target.
What are your best guesses for the main steps? Just make something up!

Smaller goal 1:	Smaller goal 2:	Smaller goal 3:
Some required steps:	Some required steps:	Some required steps:
Happy end result:	Happy end result:	Happy end result:

For each column: Star the 3 most important steps. Then circle the hardest, most confusing starred item.

What helpful limits can you apply to circled tasks, such as less research, timed sprints, or creating a simpler version?

create best guess to-dos

To Do

To generate momentum, scan What I Want and Micro-Targets.

	Monday - 14	Tuesday - 15	Wednesday - 16	Thursday - 17	Friday - 18
Appts/Errands					
Tasks (circle top 3)					
Focus Blocks					

	Saturday - 19	Sunday - 20	Must Do This Week / Notes

NOTE: There are 5 weeks this month. Fill out an extra Current Reality or Micro-Targets in the Notes section if you need to!

Truth Tracker
how your days unfold

(fill out weekly)   Date: _____

I want to go from this (current reality):   **To this (my target goal):**

[   ]   *creative tension* →   [   ]

Success Habits
1. _____
2. _____
3. _____
4. _____
5. _____

Avoidance Habits
1. _____
2. _____
3. _____
4. _____
5. _____

Daily Progress

Acorns: top 3 daily priorities. ✔ if completed or ✘ if unfinished.
Shaded rows: track each habit by # whenever it happens.

Day

Top 3 Habits

Weekend

Wins this week (despite plans):

_____

report real progress

And now, make a fresh start!

To Do

To generate momentum, scan What I Want and Micro-Targets.

	Monday - 21	Tuesday - 22	Wednesday - 23	Thursday - 24	Friday - 25
Appts/Errands					
Tasks (circle top 3)					
Focus Blocks					

Saturday - 26	Sunday - 27	Must Do This Week / Notes

Truth Tracker
how your days unfold

(fill out weekly) Date: _____

I want to go from this (current reality):

creative tension

To this (my target goal):

Success Habits
1. _____
2. _____
3. _____
4. _____
5. _____

Avoidance Habits
1. _____
2. _____
3. _____
4. _____
5. _____

Daily Progress

Acorns: top 3 daily priorities. ✔ if completed or ✘ if unfinished.
Shaded rows: track each habit by # whenever it happens.

Day

Top 3 Habits

Weekend

Wins this week (despite plans):

_____

report real progress

And now, make a fresh start!

To Do

To generate momentum,
scan What I Want and Micro-Targets.

	Monday - 28	Tuesday - 29	Wednesday - 30	Thursday - 31	Friday - 1
Appts/Errands					
Tasks (circle top 3)					
Focus Blocks					

Saturday - 2	Sunday - 3	Must Do This Week / Notes

Truth Tracker
how your days unfold

(fill out weekly)   Date: _____

I want to go from this (current reality):   *creative tension* →   **To this (my target goal):**

Success Habits
1. _____
2. _____
3. _____
4. _____
5. _____

Avoidance Habits
1. _____
2. _____
3. _____
4. _____
5. _____

Daily Progress

Acorns: top 3 daily priorities. ✓ if completed or ✗ if unfinished.
Shaded rows: track each habit by # whenever it happens.

Top 3 Habits / Weekend	Day			

Wins this week (despite plans):

_____

report real progress

And now, make a fresh start!

NOTES
Use this space to do extra check-ins and brainstorm micro-targets, along with new ideas.

capture your best ideas

NOTES

capture your best ideas

NOTES

capture your best ideas

NOTES

capture your best ideas

NOTES

PAGE #   INDEX: IMPORTANT NOTES FROM THIS MONTH

capture your best ideas

Q2 - April

PHOTO BY GRANT DURR

"So you might as well try to find the joy in creating a bad song or a bad poem or a bad painting or whatever art you need to make. We could all use a break from our egos...."
- Jeff Tweedy, How to Write One Song

What do I want to remember this month about making a fresh start, taking risks and the power of imperfection?

April Big List

Get the to-dos of your life out of your mind and onto the page. (Not in order!)

Draw new category boxes as needed. Sample categories: Health, Family, Work, Finances, Household, School, Etc.
Also: Projects, Weird Hassles, Power Hour, Fun, Friends, Pets, Decluttering, Misc.

structure the chaos

Q2 - April

Sunday	Monday	Tuesday	Wednesday	Thursday	Friday	Saturday
27	28	29	30	31	1	2
3	4	5	6	7	8	9
10	11	12	13	14	15	16
17	18	19	20	21	22	23
24	25	26	27	28	29	30
1	2	3	4	5	6	7

Notes

structure the chaos

What I Want
the vision that pulls you forward

(fill out once a quarter)

Date: _____

Describe the result you want to create in full, glorious detail!
What positive impact do you see for yourself and others?

What are the different components and how will they work? What's your ideal work rhythm? What are 1 or 2 short-term or intermediate milestones?

tap deep motivation

Target Practice
where you're going and how

(fill out once a quarter) Date: _____

I want to go from this (current reality): → *creative tension* → **To this (my target goal):**

If I knew I could have my goal, would I take it? What would I remove to make an absolute Yes!?

_____
_____
_____
_____

Work Habits
(Learn anything new? Feel free to copy from last month.)

Success	Avoidance
What previous behaviors have helped me succeed?	What previous behaviors have worked against me?

Now, circle the 5 most important behaviors in each column because you'll use them later. Well done!

cultivate courage

Current Reality
take stock and regroup

(fill out twice a month)　　　　　　　　　　　　　　　　　　　　　　Date: _____

How are you actually doing? What's going well? What's coming up that's hard to face?

What skills, advantages, relationships and resources do you have going for you?

What 3 simple steps will move you closer to your goal? Come up with a short phrase or single sentence.

manage fear

Micro-Targets
what to work on

(fill out twice a month)　　　　　　　　　　　　　　　　　　　　　Date: _____

I want to go from this (current reality):　　　　　　**To this (my target goal):**

[　　　　　　　　　　　] *creative tension* → [　　　　　　　　　　　]

Your larger goal will also have lots of little goals. Name 3 smaller goals that will help you reach your target. What are your best guesses for the main steps? Just make something up!

Smaller goal 1:	Smaller goal 2:	Smaller goal 3:
Some required steps:	Some required steps:	Some required steps:
Happy end result:	Happy end result:	Happy end result:

For each column: Star the 3 most important steps. Then circle the hardest, most confusing starred item.

What helpful limits can you apply to circled tasks, such as less research, timed sprints, or creating a simpler version?

create best guess to-dos

To Do

To generate momentum, scan What I Want and Micro-Targets.

	Monday - 4	Tuesday - 5	Wednesday - 6	Thursday - 7	Friday - 8
Appts/Errands					
Tasks (circle top 3)					
Focus Blocks					

	Saturday - 9	Sunday - 10	Must Do This Week / Notes

Truth Tracker
how your days unfold

(fill out weekly) Date: _____

I want to go from this (current reality):

[   ]

creative tension

To this (my target goal):

[   ]

Success Habits
1. _____
2. _____
3. _____
4. _____
5. _____

Avoidance Habits
1. _____
2. _____
3. _____
4. _____
5. _____

Daily Progress

Acorns: top 3 daily priorities. ✔ if completed or ✘ if unfinished.
Shaded rows: track each habit by # whenever it happens.

Day

Top 3 Habits

Weekend

Wins this week (despite plans):

_____

report real progress

And now, make a fresh start!

To Do

To generate momentum, scan What I Want and Micro-Targets.

	Monday - 11	Tuesday - 12	Wednesday - 13	Thursday - 14	Friday - 15
Appts/Errands					
Tasks (circle top 3)					
Focus Blocks					

Saturday - 16	Sunday - 17	Must Do This Week / Notes

Truth Tracker
how your days unfold

(fill out weekly)   Date: _____

I want to go from this (current reality):   *creative tension*   **To this (my target goal):**

Success Habits
1. _____
2. _____
3. _____
4. _____
5. _____

Avoidance Habits
1. _____
2. _____
3. _____
4. _____
5. _____

Daily Progress

Acorns: top 3 daily priorities. ✔ if completed or ✘ if unfinished.
Shaded rows: track each habit by # whenever it happens.

Day _____

Top 3 Habits

Weekend

Wins this week (despite plans):

_____

report real progress

And now, make a fresh start!

Current Reality
take stock and regroup

(fill out twice a month)　　　　　　　　　　　　　　　　　　　　　　　Date: _____

How are you actually doing? What's going well? What's coming up that's hard to face?

What skills, advantages, relationships and resources do you have going for you?

What 3 simple steps will move you closer to your goal? Come up with a short phrase or single sentence.

manage fear

Micro-Targets
what to work on

(fill out twice a month)　　　　　　　　　　　　　　　　　　　　　　　　Date: _____

I want to go from this (current reality):　　　　　　　　　**To this (my target goal):**

[　　　　　　　　　　　]　　*creative tension*　　[　　　　　　　　　　　]

Your larger goal will also have lots of little goals. Name 3 smaller goals that will help you reach your target.
What are your best guesses for the main steps? Just make something up!

Smaller goal 1:	Smaller goal 2:	Smaller goal 3:
Some required steps:	Some required steps:	Some required steps:
Happy end result:	Happy end result:	Happy end result:

For each column: Star the 3 most important steps. Then circle the hardest, most confusing starred item.

What helpful limits can you apply to circled tasks, such as less research, timed sprints, or creating a simpler version?

create best guess to-dos

To Do

To generate momentum, scan What I Want and Micro-Targets.

	Monday - 18	Tuesday - 19	Wednesday - 20	Thursday - 21	Friday - 22
Appts/Errands					
Tasks (circle top 3)					
Focus Blocks					

Saturday - 23	Sunday - 24	Must Do This Week / Notes

Truth Tracker
how your days unfold

(fill out weekly)   Date: _____

I want to go from this (current reality):   *creative tension* →   **To this (my target goal):**

Success Habits
1. _____
2. _____
3. _____
4. _____
5. _____

Avoidance Habits
1. _____
2. _____
3. _____
4. _____
5. _____

Daily Progress

Acorns: top 3 daily priorities. ✓ if completed or ✗ if unfinished.
Shaded rows: track each habit by # whenever it happens.

Day

Top 3 Habits

Weekend

Wins this week (despite plans):

_____

report real progress

And now, make a fresh start!

To Do

To generate momentum,
scan What I Want and Micro-Targets.

	Monday - 25	Tuesday - 26	Wednesday - 27	Thursday - 28	Friday - 29
Appts/Errands					
Tasks (circle top 3)					
Focus Blocks					

Saturday - 30	Sunday - 1	Must Do This Week / Notes

Truth Tracker
how your days unfold

(fill out weekly) Date: _____

I want to go from this (current reality):

[   ]

creative tension →

To this (my target goal):

[   ]

Success Habits
1. _____
2. _____
3. _____
4. _____
5. _____

Avoidance Habits
1. _____
2. _____
3. _____
4. _____
5. _____

Daily Progress

Acorns: top 3 daily priorities. ✓ if completed or ✗ if unfinished.
Shaded rows: track each habit by # whenever it happens.

Day

Top 3 | Habits

Weekend

Wins this week (despite plans):

_____

report real progress

And now, make a fresh start!

97

NOTES
Use this space to do extra check-ins and brainstorm micro-targets, along with new ideas.

capture your best ideas

NOTES

capture your best ideas

NOTES

capture your best ideas

NOTES

capture your best ideas

NOTES

PAGE #   INDEX: IMPORTANT NOTES FROM THIS MONTH

capture your best ideas

Q2 - May

PHOTO BY VIKTOR TALASHUK

"Most of us tend to see constraints as restrictive and adversely limiting. ...The opposite is true: they are actually fertile forces of enhancement, stimulating new possibilities."
- Adam Morgan & Mark Barden, A Beautiful Constraint

What do I want to remember this month about making a fresh start, taking risks and the power of imperfection?

May Big List

Get the to-dos of your life out of your mind and onto the page. (Not in order!)

Draw new category boxes as needed. Sample categories: Health, Family, Work, Finances, Household, School, Etc.
Also: Projects, Weird Hassles, Power Hour, Fun, Friends, Pets, Decluttering, Misc.

structure the chaos

Q2 - May

Sunday	Monday	Tuesday	Wednesday	Thursday	Friday	Saturday
1	2	3	4	5	6	7
8	9	10	11	12	13	14
15	16	17	18	19	20	21
22	23	24	25	26	27	28
29	30	31	1	2	3	4
5	6	7	8	9	10	11

Notes

structure the chaos

Current Reality

take stock and regroup

(fill out twice a month)   Date: _____

Has your big goal changed? What's going well? What's coming up that's hard to face?

What skills, advantages, relationships and resources do you have going for you?

What 3 simple steps will move you closer to your goal? Come up with a short phrase or single sentence.

manage fear

Micro-Targets
what to work on

(fill out twice a month)　　　　　　　　　　　　　　　　　　　　　Date: _____

I want to go from this (current reality):　　　　　　**To this (my target goal):**

[　　　　　　　　　　　]　*creative tension*　[　　　　　　　　　　　]

Your larger goal will also have lots of little goals. Name 3 smaller goals that will help you reach your target.
What are your best guesses for the main steps? Just make something up!

Smaller goal 1:	Smaller goal 2:	Smaller goal 3:
Some required steps:	Some required steps:	Some required steps:
Happy end result:	Happy end result:	Happy end result:

For each column: Star the 3 most important steps. Then circle the hardest, most confusing starred item.

What helpful limits can you apply to circled tasks, such as less research, timed sprints, or creating a simpler version?

create best guess to-dos

To Do

To generate momentum,
scan What I Want and Micro-Targets.

	Monday - 2	Tuesday - 3	Wednesday - 4	Thursday - 5	Friday - 6
Appts/Errands					
Tasks (circle top 3)					
Focus Blocks					

Saturday - 7	Sunday - 8	Must Do This Week / Notes

Truth Tracker

how your days unfold

(fill out weekly)   Date: _____

I want to go from this (current reality):   *creative tension*   **To this (my target goal):**

Success Habits
1. _____
2. _____
3. _____
4. _____
5. _____

Avoidance Habits
1. _____
2. _____
3. _____
4. _____
5. _____

Daily Progress

Acorns: top 3 daily priorities. ✔ if completed or ✘ if unfinished.
Shaded rows: track each habit by # whenever it happens.

Day

Top 3 Habits

Weekend

Wins this week (despite plans):

_____

_____

report real progress

And now, make a fresh start!

109

To Do

To generate momentum,
scan What I Want and Micro-Targets.

	Monday - 9	Tuesday - 10	Wednesday - 11	Thursday - 12	Friday - 13
Appts/Errands					
Tasks (circle top 3)					
Focus Blocks					

Saturday - 14	Sunday - 15	Must Do This Week / Notes

Truth Tracker
how your days unfold

(fill out weekly)   Date: _____

I want to go from this (current reality):   *creative tension*   **To this (my target goal):**

Success Habits
1. _____
2. _____
3. _____
4. _____
5. _____

Avoidance Habits
1. _____
2. _____
3. _____
4. _____
5. _____

Daily Progress

Acorns: top 3 daily priorities. ✔ if completed or ✘ if unfinished.
Shaded rows: track each habit by # whenever it happens.

Day   Habits

Top 3

Weekend

Wins this week (despite plans):

_____

report real progress   **And now, make a fresh start!**

Current Reality
take stock and regroup

(fill out twice a month) Date: _____

How are you actually doing? What's going well? What's coming up that's hard to face?

What skills, advantages, relationships and resources do you have going for you?

What 3 simple steps will move you closer to your goal? Come up with a short phrase or single sentence.

manage fear

Micro-Targets
what to work on

(fill out twice a month)　　　　　　　　　　　　　　　　　　　　　Date: _____

I want to go from this (current reality):　　　　　　　　**To this (my target goal):**

　　　[   ]　　　*creative tension*　　　[   ]

Your larger goal will also have lots of little goals. Name 3 smaller goals that will help you reach your target.
What are your best guesses for the main steps? Just make something up!

Smaller goal 1:	Smaller goal 2:	Smaller goal 3:
Some required steps:	Some required steps:	Some required steps:
Happy end result:	Happy end result:	Happy end result:

For each column: Star the 3 most important steps. Then circle the hardest, most confusing starred item.

What helpful limits can you apply to circled tasks, such as less research, timed sprints, or creating a simpler version?

create best guess to-dos

To Do

To generate momentum, scan What I Want and Micro-Targets.

	Monday - 16	Tuesday - 17	Wednesday - 18	Thursday - 19	Friday - 20
Appts/Errands					
Tasks (circle top 3)					
Focus Blocks					

Saturday - 21	Sunday - 22	Must Do This Week / Notes

Truth Tracker
how your days unfold

(fill out weekly)   Date: _____

I want to go from this (current reality):

[   ]   *creative tension* →   [   ]

To this (my target goal):

Success Habits
1. _____
2. _____
3. _____
4. _____
5. _____

Avoidance Habits
1. _____
2. _____
3. _____
4. _____
5. _____

Daily Progress

Acorns: top 3 daily priorities. ✔ if completed or ✘ if unfinished.
Shaded rows: track each habit by # whenever it happens.

Day | | |

Top 3 Habits

Weekend

Wins this week (despite plans):

_____

report real progress

And now, make a fresh start!

To Do

To generate momentum, scan What I Want and Micro-Targets.

	Monday - 23	Tuesday - 24	Wednesday - 25	Thursday - 26	Friday - 27
Appts/Errands					
Tasks (circle top 3)					
Focus Blocks					

Saturday - 28	Sunday - 29	Must Do This Week / Notes

Truth Tracker
how your days unfold

(fill out weekly)   Date: _____

I want to go from this (current reality):   **To this (my target goal):**

[current reality box   ]   *creative tension* →   [target goal box   ]

Success Habits
1. _____
2. _____
3. _____
4. _____
5. _____

Avoidance Habits
1. _____
2. _____
3. _____
4. _____
5. _____

Daily Progress

Acorns: top 3 daily priorities. ✔ if completed or ✘ if unfinished.
Shaded rows: track each habit by # whenever it happens.

Day

Top 3 Habits

Weekend

Wins this week (despite plans):

_____

report real progress

And now, make a fresh start!

NOTES
Use this space to do extra check-ins and brainstorm micro-targets, along with new ideas.

capture your best ideas

NOTES

capture your best ideas

NOTES

capture your best ideas

NOTES

capture your best ideas

NOTES

PAGE #   INDEX: IMPORTANT NOTES FROM THIS MONTH

capture your best ideas

Q2 - June

PHOTO BY MAREK LEVÁK

"Every story I create, creates me. I write to create myself."
Octavia E. Butler, science fiction writer

What do I want to remember this month about making a fresh start, taking risks and the power of imperfection?

June Big List

Get the to-dos of your life out of your mind and onto the page. (Not in order!)

Draw new category boxes as needed. Sample categories: Health, Family, Work, Finances, Household, School, Etc.
Also: Projects, Weird Hassles, Power Hour, Fun, Friends, Pets, Decluttering, Misc.

structure the chaos

Q2 - June

Sunday	Monday	Tuesday	Wednesday	Thursday	Friday	Saturday
29	30	31	1	2	3	4
5	6	7	8	9	10	11
12	13	14	15	16	17	18
19	20	21	22	23	24	25
26	27	28	29	30	1	2
3	4	5	6	7	8	9

Notes

structure the chaos

Current Reality
take stock and regroup

(fill out twice a month)　　　　　　　　　　　　　　　　　　　　Date: _____

Has your big goal changed? What's going well? What's coming up that's hard to face?

What skills, advantages, relationships and resources do you have going for you?

What 3 simple steps will move you closer to your goal? Come up with a short phrase or single sentence.

manage fear

Micro-Targets
what to work on

(fill out twice a month) Date: _____

I want to go from this (current reality):   **To this (my target goal):**

[   ] *creative tension* [   ]

Your larger goal will also have lots of little goals. Name 3 smaller goals that will help you reach your target. What are your best guesses for the main steps? Just make something up!

Smaller goal 1:	Smaller goal 2:	Smaller goal 3:
Some required steps:	Some required steps:	Some required steps:
Happy end result:	Happy end result:	Happy end result:

For each column: Star the 3 most important steps. Then circle the hardest, most confusing starred item.

What helpful limits can you apply to circled tasks, such as less research, timed sprints, or creating a simpler version?

create best guess to-dos

To Do

To generate momentum,
scan What I Want and Micro-Targets.

Monday - 30	Tuesday - 31	Wednesday - 1	Thursday - 2	Friday - 3

Appts/Errands

Tasks (circle top 3)

Focus Blocks

Saturday - 4	Sunday - 5	Must Do This Week / Notes

Truth Tracker
how your days unfold

(fill out weekly) Date: _____

I want to go from this (current reality):   *creative tension*   **To this (my target goal):**

[ ] → [ ]

Success Habits
1. _____
2. _____
3. _____
4. _____
5. _____

Avoidance Habits
1. _____
2. _____
3. _____
4. _____
5. _____

Daily Progress

Acorns: top 3 daily priorities. ✔ if completed or ✘ if unfinished.
Shaded rows: track each habit by # whenever it happens.

Day

Top 3 Habits

Weekend

Wins this week (despite plans):

_____

report real progress

And now, make a fresh start!

To Do

To generate momentum, scan What I Want and Micro-Targets.

	Monday - 6	Tuesday - 7	Wednesday - 8	Thursday - 9	Friday - 10
Appts/Errands					
Tasks (circle top 3)					
Focus Blocks					

Saturday - 11	Sunday - 12	Must Do This Week / Notes

Truth Tracker
how your days unfold

(fill out weekly) Date: _____

I want to go from this (current reality): → *creative tension* → **To this (my target goal):**

Success Habits
1. _____
2. _____
3. _____
4. _____
5. _____

Avoidance Habits
1. _____
2. _____
3. _____
4. _____
5. _____

Daily Progress

Acorns: top 3 daily priorities. ✓ if completed or ✗ if unfinished.
Shaded rows: track each habit by # whenever it happens.

Day

Top 3 Habits

Weekend

Wins this week (despite plans):

_____

report real progress

And now, make a fresh start!

Current Reality
take stock and regroup

(fill out twice a month) Date: _____

How are you actually doing? What's going well? What's coming up that's hard to face?

What skills, advantages, relationships and resources do you have going for you?

What 3 simple steps will move you closer to your goal? Come up with a short phrase or single sentence.

manage fear

Micro-Targets
what to work on

(fill out twice a month)   Date: _____

I want to go from this (current reality):   **To this (my target goal):**

[ ]   *creative tension* →   [ ]

Your larger goal will also have lots of little goals. Name 3 smaller goals that will help you reach your target.
What are your best guesses for the main steps? Just make something up!

Smaller goal 1:	Smaller goal 2:	Smaller goal 3:
Some required steps:	Some required steps:	Some required steps:
Happy end result:	Happy end result:	Happy end result:

For each column: Star the 3 most important steps. Then circle the hardest, most confusing starred item.

What helpful limits can you apply to circled tasks, such as less research, timed sprints, or creating a simpler version?

create best guess to-dos

To Do

To generate momentum, scan What I Want and Micro-Targets.

	Monday - 13	Tuesday - 14	Wednesday - 15	Thursday - 16	Friday - 17
Appts/Errands					
Tasks (circle top 3)					
Focus Blocks					

Saturday - 18	Sunday - 19	Must Do This Week / Notes
		NOTE: There are 5 weeks this month. Fill out an extra Current Reality or Micro-Targets in the Notes section if you need to!

Truth Tracker
how your days unfold

(fill out weekly) Date: _____

I want to go from this (current reality):   *creative tension*   **To this (my target goal):**

Success Habits
1. _____
2. _____
3. _____
4. _____
5. _____

Avoidance Habits
1. _____
2. _____
3. _____
4. _____
5. _____

Daily Progress
Acorns: top 3 daily priorities. ✔ if completed or ✘ if unfinished.
Shaded rows: track each habit by # whenever it happens.

Day | Top 3 Habits | Weekend

Wins this week (despite plans):

_____

report real progress

And now, make a fresh start!

To Do

To generate momentum, scan What I Want and Micro-Targets.

	Monday - 20	Tuesday - 21	Wednesday - 22	Thursday - 23	Friday - 24
Appts/Errands					
Tasks (circle top 3)					
Focus Blocks					

Saturday - 25	Sunday - 26	Must Do This Week / Notes

Truth Tracker
how your days unfold

(fill out weekly)   Date: _____

I want to go from this (current reality):   *creative tension* →   **To this (my target goal):**

Success Habits:
1. _____
2. _____
3. _____
4. _____
5. _____

Avoidance Habits:
1. _____
2. _____
3. _____
4. _____
5. _____

Daily Progress

Acorns: top 3 daily priorities. ✓ if completed or ✗ if unfinished.
Shaded rows: track each habit by # whenever it happens.

Day
Top 3 Habits

Weekend

Wins this week (despite plans):

_____

report real progress

And now, make a fresh start!

137

To Do

To generate momentum, scan What I Want and Micro-Targets.

Monday - 27	Tuesday - 28	Wednesday - 29	Thursday - 30	Friday - 1

Appts/Errands

Tasks (circle top 3)

Focus Blocks

Saturday - 2	Sunday - 3	Must Do This Week / Notes

Truth Tracker
how your days unfold

(fill out weekly) Date: _____

I want to go from this (current reality): → creative tension → **To this (my target goal):**

Success Habits
1. _____
2. _____
3. _____
4. _____
5. _____

Avoidance Habits
1. _____
2. _____
3. _____
4. _____
5. _____

Daily Progress

Acorns: top 3 daily priorities. ✔ if completed or ✘ if unfinished.
Shaded rows: track each habit by # whenever it happens.

Day

Top 3 Habits

Weekend

Wins this week (despite plans):

report real progress

And now, make a fresh start!

NOTES
Use this space to do extra check-ins and brainstorm micro-targets, along with new ideas.

capture your best ideas

NOTES

capture your best ideas

NOTES

capture your best ideas

NOTES

capture your best ideas

NOTES

PAGE #   INDEX: IMPORTANT NOTES FROM THIS MONTH

capture your best ideas

Q3 - July

PHOTO BY KÜLLI KITTUS

"The secret of the receptive must be sought in stillness.
Within stillness there remains the potential for action."
- Zhou Xuanjing, Chinese Taoist

What do I want to remember this month about making a fresh start, taking risks and the power of imperfection?

July Big List

Get the to-dos of your life out of your mind and onto the page. (Not in order!)

Draw new category boxes as needed. Sample categories: Health, Family, Work, Finances, Household, School, Etc.
Also: Projects, Weird Hassles, Power Hour, Fun, Friends, Pets, Decluttering, Misc.

structure the chaos

Q3 - July

Sunday	Monday	Tuesday	Wednesday	Thursday	Friday	Saturday
26	27	28	29	30	1	2
3	4	5	6	7	8	9
10	11	12	13	14	15	16
17	18	19	20	21	22	23
24	25	26	27	28	29	30
31	1	2	3	4	5	6

Notes

structure the chaos

What I Want
the vision that pulls you forward

(fill out once a quarter)   Date: _____

Describe the result you want to create in full, glorious detail!
What positive impact do you see for yourself and others?

What are the different components and how will they work? What's your ideal work rhythm? What are 1 or 2 short-term or intermediate milestones?

tap deep motivation

Target Practice
where you're going and how

(fill out once a quarter)   Date: _____

I want to go from this (current reality):   **To this (my target goal):**

creative tension

If I knew I could have my goal, would I take it? What would I remove to make an absolute Yes!?

_____
_____
_____
_____

Work Habits
(Learn anything new? Feel free to copy from last month.)

Success	Avoidance
What previous behaviors have helped me succeed?	What previous behaviors have worked against me?

Now, circle the 5 most important behaviors in each column because you'll use them later. Well done!

cultivate courage

Current Reality
take stock and regroup

(fill out twice a month)   Date: _____

How are you actually doing? What's going well? What's coming up that's hard to face?

What skills, advantages, relationships and resources do you have going for you?

What 3 simple steps will move you closer to your goal? Come up with a short phrase or single sentence.

manage fear

Micro-Targets
what to work on

(fill out twice a month)   Date: _____

I want to go from this (current reality):   **To this (my target goal):**

[   ]   *creative tension*   [   ]

Your larger goal will also have lots of little goals. Name 3 smaller goals that will help you reach your target.
What are your best guesses for the main steps? Just make something up!

Smaller goal 1:	Smaller goal 2:	Smaller goal 3:
Some required steps:	Some required steps:	Some required steps:
Happy end result:	Happy end result:	Happy end result:

For each column: Star the 3 most important steps. Then circle the hardest, most confusing starred item.

What helpful limits can you apply to circled tasks, such as less research, timed sprints, or creating a simpler version?

create best guess to-dos

To Do

To generate momentum, scan What I Want and Micro-Targets.

	Monday - 4	Tuesday - 5	Wednesday - 6	Thursday - 7	Friday - 8
Appts/Errands					
Tasks (circle top 3)					
Focus Blocks					

Saturday - 9	Sunday - 10	Must Do This Week / Notes

Truth Tracker
how your days unfold

(fill out weekly) Date: _____

I want to go from this (current reality):   To this (my target goal):

[_____] *creative tension* [_____]

Success Habits
1. _____
2. _____
3. _____
4. _____
5. _____

Avoidance Habits
1. _____
2. _____
3. _____
4. _____
5. _____

Daily Progress
Acorns: top 3 daily priorities. ✔ if completed or ✘ if unfinished.
Shaded rows: track each habit by # whenever it happens.

Day

Top 3 Habits

Weekend

Wins this week (despite plans):

_____

report real progress

And now, make a fresh start!

To Do

To generate momentum, scan What I Want and Micro-Targets.

	Monday - 11	Tuesday - 12	Wednesday - 13	Thursday - 14	Friday - 15
Appts/Errands					
Tasks (circle top 3)					
Focus Blocks					

Saturday - 16	Sunday - 17	Must Do This Week / Notes

Truth Tracker
how your days unfold

(fill out weekly)   Date: _____

I want to go from this (current reality):   *creative tension*   **To this (my target goal):**

Success Habits
1. _____
2. _____
3. _____
4. _____
5. _____

Avoidance Habits
1. _____
2. _____
3. _____
4. _____
5. _____

Daily Progress

Acorns: top 3 daily priorities. ✔ if completed or ✘ if unfinished.
Shaded rows: track each habit by # whenever it happens.

Day

Top 3 Habits

Weekend

Wins this week (despite plans):

_____

report real progress

And now, make a fresh start!

Current Reality
take stock and regroup

(fill out twice a month)   Date: _____

How are you actually doing? What's going well? What's coming up that's hard to face?

What skills, advantages, relationships and resources do you have going for you?

What 3 simple steps will move you closer to your goal? Come up with a short phrase or single sentence.

manage fear

Micro-Targets
what to work on

(fill out twice a month)					Date: _____

I want to go from this (current reality):			**To this (my target goal):**

[ ]   *creative tension* →   [ ]

Your larger goal will also have lots of little goals. Name 3 smaller goals that will help you reach your target.
What are your best guesses for the main steps? Just make something up!

Smaller goal 1:	Smaller goal 2:	Smaller goal 3:
Some required steps:	Some required steps:	Some required steps:
Happy end result:	Happy end result:	Happy end result:

For each column: Star the 3 most important steps. Then circle the hardest, most confusing starred item.

What helpful limits can you apply to circled tasks, such as less research, timed sprints, or creating a simpler version?

create best guess to-dos

To Do

To generate momentum,
scan What I Want and Micro-Targets.

	Monday - 18	Tuesday - 19	Wednesday - 20	Thursday - 21	Friday - 22
Appts/Errands					
Tasks (circle top 3)					
Focus Blocks					

Saturday - 23	Sunday - 24	Must Do This Week / Notes

Truth Tracker

how your days unfold

(fill out weekly) Date: _____

I want to go from this (current reality): To this (my target goal):

creative tension

Success Habits
1. _____
2. _____
3. _____
4. _____
5. _____

Avoidance Habits
1. _____
2. _____
3. _____
4. _____
5. _____

Daily Progress

Acorns: top 3 daily priorities. ✔ if completed or ✘ if unfinished.
Shaded rows: track each habit by # whenever it happens.

Day

Top 3 Habits

Weekend

Wins this week (despite plans):
_____

report real progress

And now, make a fresh start!

To Do

To generate momentum, scan What I Want and Micro-Targets.

	Monday - 25	Tuesday - 26	Wednesday - 27	Thursday - 28	Friday - 29
Appts/Errands					
Tasks (circle top 3)					
Focus Blocks					

Saturday - 30	Sunday - 31	Must Do This Week / Notes

Truth Tracker
how your days unfold

(fill out weekly) Date: _____

I want to go from this (current reality):

[ ]

creative tension →

To this (my target goal):

[ ]

Success Habits
1. _____
2. _____
3. _____
4. _____
5. _____

Avoidance Habits
1. _____
2. _____
3. _____
4. _____
5. _____

Daily Progress

Acorns: top 3 daily priorities. ✓ if completed or ✗ if unfinished.
Shaded rows: track each habit by # whenever it happens.

Day

Top 3 | Habits

Weekend

Wins this week (despite plans):

_____

report real progress

And now, make a fresh start!

161

NOTES
Use this space to do extra check-ins and brainstorm micro-targets, along with new ideas.

capture your best ideas

NOTES

capture your best ideas

NOTES

capture your best ideas

NOTES

capture your best ideas

NOTES

PAGE # INDEX: IMPORTANT NOTES FROM THIS MONTH

capture your best ideas

Q3 - August

PHOTO BY ZDENĚK MACHÁČEK

"All change comes from idiosyncratic voices."
- Seth Godin, The Practice

What do I want to remember this month about making a fresh start, taking risks and the power of imperfection?

August Big List

Get the to-dos of your life out of your mind and onto the page. (Not in order!)

Draw new category boxes as needed. Sample categories: Health, Family, Work, Finances, Household, School, Etc.
Also: Projects, Weird Hassles, Power Hour, Fun, Friends, Pets, Decluttering, Misc.

structure the chaos

Q3 - August

Sunday	Monday	Tuesday	Wednesday	Thursday	Friday	Saturday
31	1	2	3	4	5	6
7	8	9	10	11	12	13
14	15	16	17	18	19	20
21	22	23	24	25	26	27
28	29	30	31	1	2	3
4	5	6	7	8	9	10

Notes

structure the chaos

Current Reality
take stock and regroup

(fill out twice a month)　　　　　　　　　　　　　　　　　　　　　　Date: _____

Has your big goal changed? What's going well? What's coming up that's hard to face?

What skills, advantages, relationships and resources do you have going for you?

What 3 simple steps will move you closer to your goal? Come up with a short phrase or single sentence.

manage fear

Micro-Targets

what to work on

(fill out twice a month)   Date: _____

I want to go from this (current reality):   **To this (my target goal):**

creative tension

Your larger goal will also have lots of little goals. Name 3 smaller goals that will help you reach your target.
What are your best guesses for the main steps? Just make something up!

Smaller goal 1:	Smaller goal 2:	Smaller goal 3:
Some required steps:	Some required steps:	Some required steps:
Happy end result:	Happy end result:	Happy end result:

For each column: Star the 3 most important steps. Then circle the hardest, most confusing starred item.

What helpful limits can you apply to circled tasks, such as less research, timed sprints, or creating a simpler version?

create best guess to-dos

To Do

To generate momentum, scan What I Want and Micro-Targets.

	Monday - 1	Tuesday - 2	Wednesday - 3	Thursday - 4	Friday - 5
Appts/Errands					
Tasks (circle top 3)					
Focus Blocks					

Saturday - 6	Sunday - 7	Must Do This Week / Notes

Truth Tracker
how your days unfold

(fill out weekly)   Date: _____

I want to go from this (current reality):   **To this (my target goal):**

[_____]   *creative tension*   [_____]

Success Habits
1. _____
2. _____
3. _____
4. _____
5. _____

Avoidance Habits
1. _____
2. _____
3. _____
4. _____
5. _____

Daily Progress

Acorns: top 3 daily priorities. ✔ off if completed or ✘ if unfinished or not done.
Shaded rows: track each habit by # when it happens. It's fine to repeat numbers.

Day

Top 3 Habits

Weekend

Wins this week (despite plans):

_____

report real progress

And now, make a fresh start!

173

To Do

To generate momentum, scan What I Want and Micro-Targets.

	Monday - 8	Tuesday - 9	Wednesday - 10	Thursday - 11	Friday - 12
Appts/Errands					
Tasks (circle top 3)					
Focus Blocks					

Saturday - 13	Sunday - 14	Must Do This Week / Notes

Truth Tracker
how your days unfold

(fill out weekly)   Date: _____

I want to go from this (current reality):   *creative tension*   **To this (my target goal):**

Success Habits
1. _____
2. _____
3. _____
4. _____
5. _____

Avoidance Habits
1. _____
2. _____
3. _____
4. _____
5. _____

Daily Progress

Acorns: top 3 daily priorities. ✔ off if completed or ✘ if unfinished or not done.
Shaded rows: track each habit by # when it happens. It's fine to repeat numbers.

Day / *Top 3 Habits* / *Weekend*

Wins this week (despite plans):

_____

report real progress

And now, make a fresh start!

Current Reality
take stock and regroup

(fill out twice a month)

Date: _____

How are you actually doing? What's going well? What's coming up that's hard to face?

What skills, advantages, relationships and resources do you have going for you?

What 3 simple steps will move you closer to your goal? Come up with a short phrase or single sentence.

manage fear

Micro-Targets
what to work on

(fill out twice a month)　　　　　　　　　　　　　　　　　　　　　　　Date: _____

I want to go from this (current reality):　　　　　　　　**To this (my target goal):**

　　　[   ]　　　*creative tension*　　　[   ]

Your larger goal will also have lots of little goals. Name 3 smaller goals that will help you reach your target.
What are your best guesses for the main steps? Just make something up!

Smaller goal 1:	Smaller goal 2:	Smaller goal 3:
Some required steps:	Some required steps:	Some required steps:
Happy end result:	Happy end result:	Happy end result:

For each column: Star the 3 most important steps. Then circle the hardest, most confusing starred item.

What helpful limits can you apply to circled tasks, such as less research, timed sprints, or creating a simpler version?

create best guess to-dos

To Do

To generate momentum, scan What I Want and Micro-Targets.

	Monday - 15	Tuesday - 16	Wednesday - 17	Thursday - 18	Friday - 19
Appts/Errands					
Tasks (circle top 3)					
Focus Blocks					

Saturday - 20	Sunday - 21	Must Do This Week / Notes
		NOTE: There are 5 weeks this month. Fill out an extra Current Reality or Micro-Targets in the Notes section if you need to!

Truth Tracker
how your days unfold

(fill out weekly) Date: _____

I want to go from this (current reality): → *creative tension* **To this (my target goal):**

Success Habits:
1. _____
2. _____
3. _____
4. _____
5. _____

Avoidance Habits:
1. _____
2. _____
3. _____
4. _____
5. _____

Daily Progress

Acorns: top 3 daily priorities. ✔ off if completed or ✘ if unfinished or not done.
Shaded rows: track each habit by # when it happens. It's fine to repeat numbers.

Day

Top 3 Habits

Weekend

Wins this week (despite plans):

_____

_____

report real progress

And now, make a fresh start!

179

To Do

To generate momentum, scan What I Want and Micro-Targets.

	Monday - 22	Tuesday - 23	Wednesday - 24	Thursday - 25	Friday - 26
Appts/Errands					
Tasks (circle top 3)					
Focus Blocks					

	Saturday - 27	Sunday - 28	Must Do This Week / Notes

Truth Tracker
how your days unfold

(fill out weekly)   Date: _____

I want to go from this (current reality):   **To this (my target goal):**

[   ]   *creative tension*   [   ]

Success Habits
1. _____
2. _____
3. _____
4. _____
5. _____

Avoidance Habits
1. _____
2. _____
3. _____
4. _____
5. _____

Daily Progress

Acorns: top 3 daily priorities. ✓ off if completed or ✗ if unfinished or not done.
Shaded rows: track each habit by # when it happens. It's fine to repeat numbers.

Day

Top 3 Habits

Weekend

Wins this week (despite plans):

_____

_____

report real progress

And now, make a fresh start!

To Do

To generate momentum, scan What I Want and Micro-Targets.

	Monday - 29	Tuesday - 30	Wednesday - 31	Thursday - 1	Friday - 2
Appts/Errands					
Tasks (circle top 3)					
Focus Blocks					

Saturday - 3	Sunday - 4	Must Do This Week / Notes

Truth Tracker
how your days unfold

(fill out weekly)   Date: _____

I want to go from this (current reality):   **To this (my target goal):**

[   ]   *creative tension*   [   ]

Success Habits
1. _____
2. _____
3. _____
4. _____
5. _____

Avoidance Habits
1. _____
2. _____
3. _____
4. _____
5. _____

Daily Progress

Acorns: top 3 daily priorities. ✔ off if completed or ✘ if unfinished or not done.
Shaded rows: track each habit by # when it happens. It's fine to repeat numbers.

Day

Top 3 Habits

Weekend

Wins this week (despite plans):

_____

report real progress

And now, make a fresh start!

NOTES
Use this space to do extra check-ins and brainstorm micro-targets, along with new ideas.

capture your best ideas

NOTES

capture your best ideas

NOTES

capture your best ideas

NOTES

capture your best ideas

NOTES

PAGE #   INDEX: IMPORTANT NOTES FROM THIS MONTH

capture your best ideas

Q3 - September

PHOTO BY FOX

"What I have realized through practicing is that practice isn't about being the best horse or the good horse or the poor horse or the worst horse. It's about finding our own true nature and speaking from that, acting from that."
- Pema Chödrön, Buddhist nun

What do I want to remember this month about making a fresh start, taking risks and the power of imperfection?

September Big List

Get the to-dos of your life out of your mind and onto the page. (Not in order!)

Draw new category boxes as needed. Sample categories: Health, Family, Work, Finances, Household, School, Etc.
Also: Projects, Weird Hassles, Power Hour, Fun, Friends, Pets, Decluttering, Misc.

structure the chaos

Q3 - September

Sunday	Monday	Tuesday	Wednesday	Thursday	Friday	Saturday
28	29	30	31	1	2	3
4	5	6	7	8	9	10
11	12	13	14	15	16	17
18	19	20	21	22	23	24
25	26	27	28	29	30	1
2	3	4	5	6	7	8

Notes

structure the chaos

Current Reality
take stock and regroup

(fill out twice a month) Date: _____

Has your big goal changed? What's going well? What's coming up that's hard to face?

_____
_____
_____
_____
_____
_____
_____
_____
_____
_____
_____
_____
_____

What skills, advantages, relationships and resources do you have going for you?

_____
_____
_____
_____

What 3 simple steps will move you closer to your goal? Come up with a short phrase or single sentence.

manage fear

Micro-Targets
what to work on

(fill out twice a month)   Date: _____

I want to go from this (current reality):   **To this (my target goal):**

[   ]   *creative tension* →   [   ]

Your larger goal will also have lots of little goals. Name 3 smaller goals that will help you reach your target.
What are your best guesses for the main steps? Just make something up!

Smaller goal 1:	Smaller goal 2:	Smaller goal 3:
Some required steps:	Some required steps:	Some required steps:
Happy end result:	Happy end result:	Happy end result:

For each column: Star the 3 most important steps. Then circle the hardest, most confusing starred item.

What helpful limits can you apply to circled tasks, such as less research, timed sprints, or creating a simpler version?

create best guess to-dos

To Do

To generate momentum, scan What I Want and Micro-Targets.

	Monday - 5	Tuesday - 6	Wednesday - 7	Thursday - 8	Friday - 9
Appts/Errands					
Tasks (circle top 3)					
Focus Blocks					

	Saturday - 10	Sunday - 11	Must Do This Week / Notes

Truth Tracker
how your days unfold

(fill out weekly)　　　　　　　　　　　　　　　　　　　　　　　　Date: _____

I want to go from this (current reality):　　　*creative tension*　　　**To this (my target goal):**

Success Habits
1. _____
2. _____
3. _____
4. _____
5. _____

Avoidance Habits
1. _____
2. _____
3. _____
4. _____
5. _____

Daily Progress

Acorns: top 3 daily priorities. ✓ if completed or ✗ if unfinished.
Shaded rows: track each habit by # whenever it happens.

Day

Top 3 Habits

Weekend

Wins this week (despite plans):

_____

report real progress

And now, make a fresh start!

To Do

To generate momentum, scan What I Want and Micro-Targets.

	Monday - 12	Tuesday - 13	Wednesday - 14	Thursday - 15	Friday - 16
Appts/Errands					
Tasks (circle top 3)					
Focus Blocks					

Saturday - 17	Sunday - 18	Must Do This Week / Notes

Truth Tracker
how your days unfold

(fill out weekly)   Date: _____

I want to go from this (current reality):   **To this (my target goal):**

[current reality box]   *creative tension*   [target goal box]

Success Habits
1. _____
2. _____
3. _____
4. _____
5. _____

Avoidance Habits
1. _____
2. _____
3. _____
4. _____
5. _____

Daily Progress

Acorns: top 3 daily priorities. ✔ if completed or ✘ if unfinished.
Shaded rows: track each habit by # whenever it happens.

Day

Top 3 Habits

Weekend

Wins this week (despite plans):

_____

report real progress

And now, make a fresh start!

Current Reality
take stock and regroup

(fill out twice a month)　　　　　　　　　　　　　　　　　　　　　　Date: _____

How are you actually doing? What's going well? What's coming up that's hard to face?

What skills, advantages, relationships and resources do you have going for you?

What 3 simple steps will move you closer to your goal? Come up with a short phrase or single sentence.

manage fear

Micro-Targets
what to work on

(fill out twice a month)

Date: _____

I want to go from this (current reality):

To this (my target goal):

creative tension

Your larger goal will also have lots of little goals. Name 3 smaller goals that will help you reach your target.
What are your best guesses for the main steps? Just make something up!

Smaller goal 1:	Smaller goal 2:	Smaller goal 3:
Some required steps:	Some required steps:	Some required steps:
Happy end result:	Happy end result:	Happy end result:

For each column: Star the 3 most important steps. Then circle the hardest, most confusing starred item.

What helpful limits can you apply to circled tasks, such as less research, timed sprints, or creating a simpler version?

create best guess to-dos

To Do

To generate momentum,
scan What I Want and Micro-Targets.

	Monday - 19	Tuesday - 20	Wednesday - 21	Thursday - 22	Friday - 23
Appts/Errands					
Tasks (circle top 3)					
Focus Blocks					

Saturday - 24	Sunday - 25	Must Do This Week / Notes

Truth Tracker
how your days unfold

(fill out weekly)   Date: _____

I want to go from this (current reality):   **To this (my target goal):**

[   ]   *creative tension* →   [   ]

Success Habits
1. _____
2. _____
3. _____
4. _____
5. _____

Avoidance Habits
1. _____
2. _____
3. _____
4. _____
5. _____

Daily Progress

Acorns: top 3 daily priorities. ✔ if completed or ✘ if unfinished.
Shaded rows: track each habit by # whenever it happens.

Day			
Top 3 Habits	🌰	🌰	🌰
	🌰	🌰	🌰
	🌰	🌰	🌰
	🌰	🌰	🌰
	🌰	🌰	🌰
Weekend	🌰	🌰	🌰

Wins this week (despite plans):

_____

report real progress   **And now, make a fresh start!**

To Do

To generate momentum, scan What I Want and Micro-Targets.

	Monday - 26	Tuesday - 27	Wednesday - 28	Thursday - 29	Friday - 30
Appts/Errands					
Tasks (circle top 3)					
Focus Blocks					

	Saturday - 1	Sunday - 2	Must Do This Week / Notes

Truth Tracker
how your days unfold

(fill out weekly)   Date: _____

I want to go from this (current reality):   *creative tension* →   **To this (my target goal):**

Success Habits
1. _____
2. _____
3. _____
4. _____
5. _____

Avoidance Habits
1. _____
2. _____
3. _____
4. _____
5. _____

Daily Progress

Acorns: top 3 daily priorities. ✓ if completed or ✗ if unfinished.
Shaded rows: track each habit by # whenever it happens.

Day | Top 3 Habits | Weekend

Wins this week (despite plans):

_____

_____

report real progress

And now, make a fresh start!

NOTES
Use this space to do extra check-ins and brainstorm micro-targets, along with new ideas.

capture your best ideas

NOTES

capture your best ideas

NOTES

capture your best ideas

NOTES

capture your best ideas

NOTES

PAGE #	INDEX: IMPORTANT NOTES FROM THIS MONTH

capture your best ideas

Q4 - October

PHOTO BY WŁODZIMIERZ JAWORSKI

"You may have a fresh start any moment you choose, for this thing that we call 'failure' is not the falling down, but the staying down."
- Mary Pickford

What do I want to remember this month about making a fresh start, taking risks and the power of imperfection?

October Big List

Get the to-dos of your life out of your mind and onto the page. (Not in order!)

Draw new category boxes as needed. Sample categories: Health, Family, Work, Finances, Household, School, Etc.
Also: Projects, Weird Hassles, Power Hour, Fun, Friends, Pets, Decluttering, Misc.

structure the chaos

Q4 - October

Sunday	Monday	Tuesday	Wednesday	Thursday	Friday	Saturday
25	26	27	28	29	30	1
2	3	4	5	6	7	8
9	10	11	12	13	14	15
16	17	18	19	20	21	22
23	24	25	26	27	28	29
30	31	1	2	3	4	5

Notes

structure the chaos

What I Want
the vision that pulls you forward

(fill out once a quarter) Date: _____

Describe the result you want to create in full, glorious detail!
What positive impact do you see for yourself and others?

What are the different components and how will they work? What's your ideal work rhythm? What are 1 or 2 short-term or intermediate milestones?

tap deep motivation

Target Practice
where you're going and how

(fill out once a quarter)

Date: _____

I want to go from this (current reality):

To this (my target goal):

creative tension

If I knew I could have my goal, would I take it? What would I remove to make an absolute Yes!?

_____
_____
_____
_____
_____

Work Habits
(Learn anything new? Feel free to copy from last month.)

Success	Avoidance
What previous behaviors have helped me succeed?	What previous behaviors have worked against me?

Now, circle the 5 most important behaviors in each column because you'll use them later. Well done!

cultivate courage

Current Reality
take stock and regroup

(fill out twice a month)   Date: _____

How are you actually doing? What's going well? What's coming up that's hard to face?

What skills, advantages, relationships and resources do you have going for you?

What 3 simple steps will move you closer to your goal? Come up with a short phrase or single sentence.

manage fear

Micro-Targets
what to work on

(fill out twice a month)   Date: _____

I want to go from this (current reality):   **To this (my target goal):**

[   ]   *creative tension*   [   ]

Your larger goal will also have lots of little goals. Name 3 smaller goals that will help you reach your target.
What are your best guesses for the main steps? Just make something up!

Smaller goal 1:	Smaller goal 2:	Smaller goal 3:
Some required steps:	Some required steps:	Some required steps:
Happy end result:	Happy end result:	Happy end result:

For each column: Star the 3 most important steps. Then circle the hardest, most confusing starred item.

What helpful limits can you apply to circled tasks, such as less research, timed sprints, or creating a simpler version?

create best guess to-dos

To Do

To generate momentum, scan What I Want and Micro-Targets.

	Monday - 3	Tuesday - 4	Wednesday - 5	Thursday - 6	Friday - 7
Appts/Errands					
Tasks (circle top 3)					
Focus Blocks					

Saturday - 8	Sunday - 9	Must Do This Week / Notes

Truth Tracker
how your days unfold

(fill out weekly)   Date: _____

I want to go from this (current reality):   **To this (my target goal):**

[box]   *creative tension*   [box]

Success Habits
1. _____
2. _____
3. _____
4. _____
5. _____

Avoidance Habits
1. _____
2. _____
3. _____
4. _____
5. _____

Daily Progress

Acorns: top 3 daily priorities. ✔ if completed or ✘ if unfinished.
Shaded rows: track each habit by # whenever it happens.

Day

Top 3 Habits

Weekend

Wins this week (despite plans):

_____

report real progress

And now, make a fresh start!

To Do

To generate momentum, scan What I Want and Micro-Targets.

	Monday - 10	Tuesday - 11	Wednesday - 12	Thursday - 13	Friday - 14
Appts/Errands					
Tasks (circle top 3)					
Focus Blocks					

	Saturday - 15	Sunday - 16	Must Do This Week / Notes

Truth Tracker
how your days unfold

(fill out weekly)   Date: _____

I want to go from this (current reality):   **To this (my target goal):**

[ ] → creative tension → [ ]

Success Habits
1. _____
2. _____
3. _____
4. _____
5. _____

Avoidance Habits
1. _____
2. _____
3. _____
4. _____
5. _____

Daily Progress

Acorns: top 3 daily priorities. ✓ if completed or ✗ if unfinished.
Shaded rows: track each habit by # whenever it happens.

Day

Top 3 Habits

Weekend

Wins this week (despite plans):

_____

And now, make a fresh start!

report real progress

Current Reality
take stock and regroup

(fill out twice a month)   Date: _____

How are you actually doing? What's going well? What's coming up that's hard to face?

What skills, advantages, relationships and resources do you have going for you?

What 3 simple steps will move you closer to your goal? Come up with a short phrase or single sentence.

manage fear

Micro-Targets
what to work on

(fill out twice a month)   Date: _____

I want to go from this (current reality):   **To this (my target goal):**

creative tension

Your larger goal will also have lots of little goals. Name 3 smaller goals that will help you reach your target. What are your best guesses for the main steps? Just make something up!

Smaller goal 1:	Smaller goal 2:	Smaller goal 3:
Some required steps:	Some required steps:	Some required steps:
Happy end result:	Happy end result:	Happy end result:

For each column: Star the 3 most important steps. Then circle the hardest, most confusing starred item.

What helpful limits can you apply to circled tasks, such as less research, timed sprints, or creating a simpler version?

create best guess to-dos

To Do

To generate momentum,
scan What I Want and Micro-Targets.

	Monday - 17	Tuesday - 18	Wednesday - 19	Thursday - 20	Friday - 21
Appts/Errands					
Tasks (circle top 3)					
Focus Blocks					

Saturday - 22	Sunday - 23	Must Do This Week / Notes

Truth Tracker
how your days unfold

(fill out weekly)   Date: _____

I want to go from this (current reality):   **To this (my target goal):**

[current reality box   ]   →*creative tension*→   [target goal box   ]

Success Habits
1. _____
2. _____
3. _____
4. _____
5. _____

Avoidance Habits
1. _____
2. _____
3. _____
4. _____
5. _____

Daily Progress

Acorns: top 3 daily priorities. ✔ if completed or ✘ if unfinished.
Shaded rows: track each habit by # whenever it happens.

Day / Top 3 Habits / Weekend

Wins this week (despite plans):
_____

report real progress

And now, make a fresh start!

To Do

To generate momentum, scan What I Want and Micro-Targets.

	Monday - 24	Tuesday - 25	Wednesday - 26	Thursday - 27	Friday - 28
Appts/Errands					
Tasks (circle top 3)					
Focus Blocks					

Saturday - 29	Sunday - 30	Must Do This Week / Notes

Truth Tracker

how your days unfold

(fill out weekly)   Date: _____

I want to go from this (current reality):   *creative tension* →   **To this (my target goal):**

[current reality box]   [target goal box]

Success Habits
1. _____
2. _____
3. _____
4. _____
5. _____

Avoidance Habits
1. _____
2. _____
3. _____
4. _____
5. _____

Daily Progress

Acorns: top 3 daily priorities. ✓ if completed or ✗ if unfinished.
Shaded rows: track each habit by # whenever it happens.

	Day		
Top 3 Habits	🌰	🌰	🌰
	🌰	🌰	🌰
	🌰	🌰	🌰
	🌰	🌰	🌰
	🌰	🌰	🌰
Weekend			
	🌰	🌰	🌰

Wins this week (despite plans):

_____

report real progress   **And now, make a fresh start!**

NOTES
Use this space to do extra check-ins and brainstorm micro-targets, along with new ideas.

capture your best ideas

NOTES

capture your best ideas

NOTES

capture your best ideas

NOTES

capture your best ideas

NOTES

PAGE # | INDEX: IMPORTANT NOTES FROM THIS MONTH

capture your best ideas

Q4 - November

PHOTO BY ZDENĚK MACHÁČEK

"The acquisition of knowledge always involves
the revelation of ignorance...."
- Wendell Berry, Standing by Words

What do I want to remember this month about making a fresh start, taking risks and the power of imperfection?

November Big List

Get the to-dos of your life out of your mind and onto the page. (Not in order!)

Draw new category boxes as needed. Sample categories: Health, Family, Work, Finances, Household, School, Etc.
Also: Projects, Weird Hassles, Power Hour, Fun, Friends, Pets, Decluttering, Misc.

structure the chaos

Q4 - November

Sunday	Monday	Tuesday	Wednesday	Thursday	Friday	Saturday
30	31	1	2	3	4	5
6	7	8	9	10	11	12
13	14	15	15	17	18	19
20	21	22	23	24	25	26
27	28	29	30	1	2	3
4	5	6	7	8	9	10

Notes

structure the chaos

Current Reality

take stock and regroup

(fill out twice a month) Date: _____

Has your big goal changed? What's going well? What's coming up that's hard to face?

What skills, advantages, relationships and resources do you have going for you?

What 3 simple steps will move you closer to your goal? Come up with a short phrase or single sentence.

manage fear

Micro-Targets
what to work on

(fill out twice a month)　　　　　　　　　　　　　　　　　　　　　Date: _____

I want to go from this (current reality):　　　　　　　**To this (my target goal):**

[   ]　　*creative tension*　　[   ]

Your larger goal will also have lots of little goals. Name 3 smaller goals that will help you reach your target.
What are your best guesses for the main steps? Just make something up!

Smaller goal 1:	Smaller goal 2:	Smaller goal 3:
Some required steps:	Some required steps:	Some required steps:
Happy end result:	Happy end result:	Happy end result:

For each column: Star the 3 most important steps. Then circle the hardest, most confusing starred item.

What helpful limits can you apply to circled tasks, such as less research, timed sprints, or creating a simpler version?

create best guess to-dos

235

To Do

To generate momentum, scan What I Want and Micro-Targets.

	Monday - 31	Tuesday - 1	Wednesday - 2	Thursday - 3	Friday - 4
Appts/Errands					
Tasks (circle top 3)					
Focus Blocks					

Saturday - 5	Sunday - 6	Must Do This Week / Notes

Truth Tracker
how your days unfold

(fill out weekly)   Date: _____

I want to go from this (current reality):   *creative tension*   **To this (my target goal):**

Success Habits
1. _____
2. _____
3. _____
4. _____
5. _____

Avoidance Habits
1. _____
2. _____
3. _____
4. _____
5. _____

Daily Progress

Acorns: top 3 daily priorities. ✔ if completed or ✘ if unfinished.
Shaded rows: track each habit by # whenever it happens.

Day / **Top 3 Habits** / **Weekend**

Wins this week (despite plans):

_____

report real progress

And now, make a fresh start!

To Do

To generate momentum, scan What I Want and Micro-Targets.

	Monday - 7	Tuesday - 8	Wednesday - 9	Thursday - 10	Friday - 11
Appts/Errands					
Tasks (circle top 3)					
Focus Blocks					

Saturday - 12	Sunday - 13	Must Do This Week / Notes

Truth Tracker

how your days unfold

(fill out weekly)   Date: _____

I want to go from this (current reality):   *creative tension*   **To this (my target goal):**

Success Habits:
1. _____
2. _____
3. _____
4. _____
5. _____

Avoidance Habits:
1. _____
2. _____
3. _____
4. _____
5. _____

Daily Progress

Acorns: top 3 daily priorities. ✔ if completed or ✘ if unfinished.
Shaded rows: track each habit by # whenever it happens.

Day | Top 3 Habits | Weekend

Wins this week (despite plans):

report real progress

And now, make a fresh start!

239

Current Reality
take stock and regroup

(fill out twice a month)　　　　　　　　　　　　　　　　　　　Date: _____

How are you actually doing? What's going well? What's coming up that's hard to face?

What skills, advantages, relationships and resources do you have going for you?

What 3 simple steps will move you closer to your goal? Come up with a short phrase or single sentence.

manage fear

Micro-Targets
what to work on

(fill out twice a month) Date: _____

I want to go from this (current reality): **To this (my target goal):**

creative tension

Your larger goal will also have lots of little goals. Name 3 smaller goals that will help you reach your target.
What are your best guesses for the main steps? Just make something up!

Smaller goal 1:	Smaller goal 2:	Smaller goal 3:
Some required steps:	Some required steps:	Some required steps:
Happy end result:	Happy end result:	Happy end result:

For each column: Star the 3 most important steps. Then circle the hardest, most confusing starred item.

What helpful limits can you apply to circled tasks, such as less research, timed sprints, or creating a simpler version?

create best guess to-dos

To Do

To generate momentum, scan What I Want and Micro-Targets.

	Monday - 14	Tuesday - 15	Wednesday - 16	Thursday - 17	Friday - 18
Appts/Errands					
Tasks (circle top 3)					
Focus Blocks					

Saturday - 19	Sunday - 20	Must Do This Week / Notes
		NOTE: There are 5 weeks this month. Fill out an extra Current Reality or Micro-Targets in the Notes section if you need to!

Truth Tracker
how your days unfold

(fill out weekly) Date: _____

I want to go from this (current reality):

[ ] → *creative tension* → **To this (my target goal):** [ ]

Success Habits
1. _____
2. _____
3. _____
4. _____
5. _____

Avoidance Habits
1. _____
2. _____
3. _____
4. _____
5. _____

Daily Progress
Acorns: top 3 daily priorities. ✔ if completed or ✘ if unfinished.
Shaded rows: track each habit by # whenever it happens.

Day | | |
Top 3 Habits

(Weekend)

Wins this week (despite plans):
_____

report real progress

And now, make a fresh start!

To Do

To generate momentum, scan What I Want and Micro-Targets.

	Monday - 21	Tuesday - 22	Wednesday - 23	Thursday - 24	Friday - 25
Appts/Errands					
Tasks (circle top 3)					
Focus Blocks					

Saturday - 26	Sunday - 27	Must Do This Week / Notes

Truth Tracker
how your days unfold

(fill out weekly)　　　　　　　　　　　　　　　　　　　　　　　　　　　Date: _____

I want to go from this (current reality):　　　　　　　To this (my target goal):

　　　　　　　　　　　　　　　　　　creative tension

Success Habits
1. _____
2. _____
3. _____
4. _____
5. _____

Avoidance Habits
1. _____
2. _____
3. _____
4. _____
5. _____

Daily Progress

Acorns: top 3 daily priorities. ✓ if completed or ✗ if unfinished.
Shaded rows: track each habit by # whenever it happens.

Day

Top 3 Habits

Weekend

Wins this week (despite plans):

_____

report real progress

And now, make a fresh start!

To Do

To generate momentum, scan What I Want and Micro-Targets.

	Monday - 28	Tuesday - 29	Wednesday - 30	Thursday - 1	Friday - 2
Appts/Errands					
Tasks (circle top 3)					
Focus Blocks					

Saturday - 3	Sunday - 4	Must Do This Week / Notes

Truth Tracker

how your days unfold

(fill out weekly)

Date: ____________

I want to go from this (current reality):

To this (my target goal):

creative tension

Success Habits

1. ____________
2. ____________
3. ____________
4. ____________
5. ____________

Avoidance Habits

1. ____________
2. ____________
3. ____________
4. ____________
5. ____________

Daily Progress

Acorns: top 3 daily priorities. ✔ if completed or ✘ if unfinished.
Shaded rows: track each habit by # whenever it happens.

Day		
Habits		
Top 3		
Weekend		

Wins this week (despite plans):

____

____

And now,
make a fresh start!

report real progress

NOTES
Use this space to do extra check-ins and brainstorm micro-targets, along with new ideas.

capture your best ideas

NOTES

capture your best ideas

NOTES

capture your best ideas

NOTES

capture your best ideas

NOTES

PAGE #   INDEX: IMPORTANT NOTES FROM THIS MONTH

capture your best ideas

Q4 - December

PHOTO BY DUŠAN VEVERKOLOG

"To be gritty is to keep putting one foot in front of the other. ...To hold fast to an interesting and purposeful goal. ...To invest, day after week after year, in challenging practice."
- Angela Duckworth, Grit

What do I want to remember this month about making a fresh start, taking risks and the power of imperfection?

December Big List

Get the to-dos of your life out of your mind and onto the page. (Not in order!)

Draw new category boxes as needed. Sample categories: Health, Family, Work, Finances, Household, School, Etc.
Also: Projects, Weird Hassles, Power Hour, Fun, Friends, Pets, Decluttering, Misc.

structure the chaos

Q4 - December

Sunday	Monday	Tuesday	Wednesday	Thursday	Friday	Saturday
27	28	29	30	1	2	3
4	5	6	7	8	9	10
11	12	13	14	15	16	17
18	19	20	21	22	23	24
25	26	27	28	29	30	1
2	3	4	5	6	7	8

Notes

structure the chaos

Current Reality
take stock and regroup

(fill out twice a month)   Date: _____

Has your big goal changed? What's going well? What's coming up that's hard to face?

What skills, advantages, relationships and resources do you have going for you?

What 3 simple steps will move you closer to your goal? Come up with a short phrase or single sentence.

manage fear

Micro-Targets
what to work on

(fill out twice a month) Date: _____

I want to go from this (current reality):   **To this (my target goal):**

creative tension

Your larger goal will also have lots of little goals. Name 3 smaller goals that will help you reach your target. What are your best guesses for the main steps? Just make something up!

Smaller goal 1: Smaller goal 2: Smaller goal 3:

Some required steps: Some required steps: Some required steps:

Happy end result: Happy end result: Happy end result:

For each column: Star the 3 most important steps. Then circle the hardest, most confusing starred item.

What helpful limits can you apply to circled tasks, such as less research, timed sprints, or creating a simpler version?

create best guess to-dos

To Do

To generate momentum, scan What I Want and Micro-Targets.

	Monday - 5	Tuesday - 6	Wednesday - 7	Thursday - 8	Friday - 9
Appts/Errands					
Tasks (circle top 3)					
Focus Blocks					

Saturday - 10	Sunday - 11	Must Do This Week / Notes

Truth Tracker
how your days unfold

(fill out weekly)　　　　　　　　　　　　　　　　　　　　　　Date: _____

I want to go from this (current reality):　　　　　*creative tension*　　　　**To this (my target goal):**

Success Habits:
1. _____
2. _____
3. _____
4. _____
5. _____

Avoidance Habits:
1. _____
2. _____
3. _____
4. _____
5. _____

Daily Progress

Acorns: top 3 daily priorities. ✓ off if completed or ✗ if unfinished or not done.
Shaded rows: track each habit by # when it happens. It's fine to repeat numbers.

Day / Top 3 Habits / Weekend

Wins this week (despite plans):

_____

report real progress

And now, make a fresh start!

To Do

To generate momentum, scan What I Want and Micro-Targets.

	Monday - 12	Tuesday - 13	Wednesday - 14	Thursday - 15	Friday - 16
Appts/Errands					
Tasks (circle top 3)					
Focus Blocks					

Saturday - 17	Sunday - 18	Must Do This Week / Notes

Truth Tracker
how your days unfold

(fill out weekly) Date: _____

I want to go from this (current reality):

[   ]

creative tension

To this (my target goal):

[   ]

Success Habits
1. _____
2. _____
3. _____
4. _____
5. _____

Avoidance Habits
1. _____
2. _____
3. _____
4. _____
5. _____

Daily Progress

Acorns: top 3 daily priorities. ✓ off if completed or ✗ if unfinished or not done.
Shaded rows: track each habit by # when it happens. It's fine to repeat numbers.

Day | | |

Top 3 Habits

Weekend

Wins this week (despite plans):

_____

_____

report real progress

And now, make a fresh start!

Current Reality
take stock and regroup

(fill out twice a month)　　　　　　　　　　　　　　　　　　　Date: _____

How are you actually doing? What's going well? What's coming up that's hard to face?

What skills, advantages, relationships and resources do you have going for you?

What 3 simple steps will move you closer to your goal? Come up with a short phrase or single sentence.

manage fear

Micro-Targets
what to work on

(fill out twice a month)　　　　　　　　　　　　　　　　　　　　　　Date: _____

I want to go from this (current reality):　　　　　　　　**To this (my target goal):**

[_____]　　*creative tension* →　　[_____]

Your larger goal will also have lots of little goals. Name 3 smaller goals that will help you reach your target.
What are your best guesses for the main steps? Just make something up!

Smaller goal 1:	Smaller goal 2:	Smaller goal 3:
Some required steps:	Some required steps:	Some required steps:
Happy end result:	Happy end result:	Happy end result:

For each column: Star the 3 most important steps. Then circle the hardest, most confusing starred item.

What helpful limits can you apply to circled tasks, such as less research, timed sprints, or creating a simpler version?

create best guess to-dos

To Do

To generate momentum,
scan What I Want and Micro-Targets.

	Monday - 19	Tuesday - 20	Wednesday - 21	Thursday - 22	Friday - 23
Appts/Errands					
Tasks (circle top 3)					
Focus Blocks					

Saturday - 24	Sunday - 25	Must Do This Week / Notes

Truth Tracker
how your days unfold

(fill out weekly) Date: _____

I want to go from this (current reality):

[   ]   *creative tension*   **To this (my target goal):**

[   ]

Success Habits
1. _____
2. _____
3. _____
4. _____
5. _____

Avoidance Habits
1. _____
2. _____
3. _____
4. _____
5. _____

Daily Progress

Acorns: top 3 daily priorities. ✓ off if completed or ✗ if unfinished or not done.
Shaded rows: track each habit by # when it happens. It's fine to repeat numbers.

Day

Top 3 Habits

Weekend

Wins this week (despite plans):

_____

report real progress

And now, make a fresh start!

To Do

To generate momentum, scan What I Want and Micro-Targets.

	Monday - 26	Tuesday - 27	Wednesday - 28	Thursday - 29	Friday - 30
Appts/Errands					
Tasks (circle top 3)					
Focus Blocks					

Saturday - 31	Sunday - 1 (2023)	Must Do This Week / Notes

Truth Tracker
how your days unfold

(fill out weekly)   Date: _____

I want to go from this (current reality):   *creative tension*   **To this (my target goal):**

Success Habits
1. _____
2. _____
3. _____
4. _____
5. _____

Avoidance Habits
1. _____
2. _____
3. _____
4. _____
5. _____

Daily Progress

Acorns: top 3 daily priorities. ✔ off if completed or ✘ if unfinished or not done.
Shaded rows: track each habit by # when it happens. It's fine to repeat numbers.

Day

Top 3 Habits

Weekend

Wins this week (despite plans):
_____
_____

report real progress

And now, make a fresh start!

NOTES
Use this space to do extra check-ins and brainstorm micro-targets, along with new ideas.

capture your best ideas

NOTES

capture your best ideas

NOTES

capture your best ideas

NOTES

capture your best ideas

NOTES

PAGE #   INDEX: IMPORTANT NOTES FROM THIS MONTH

capture your best ideas

PHOTO BY DAN ROIZER

04

Resolve Mysterious Setbacks

Troubleshooting tips

How everything ties together

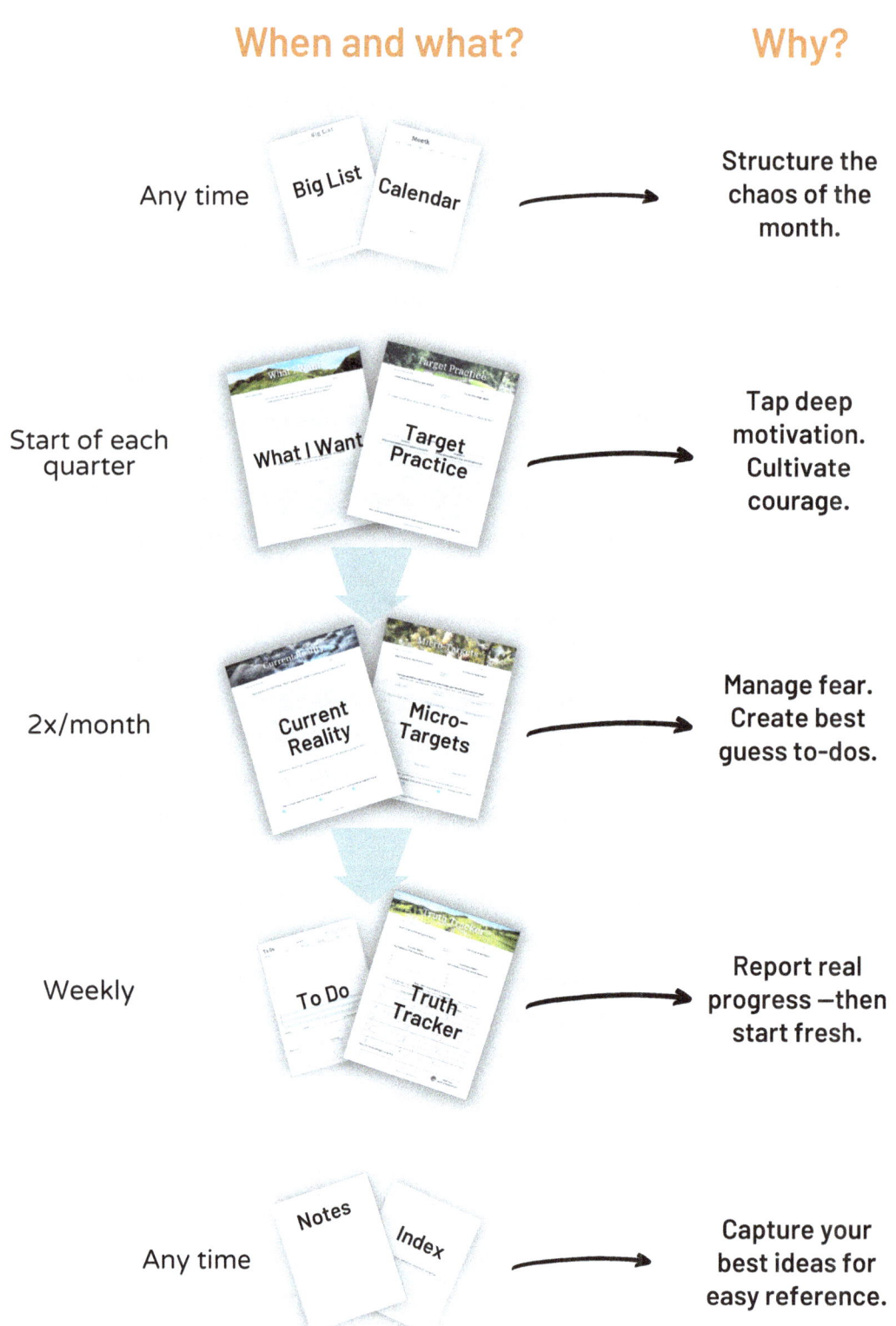

Troubleshooting tips

When you're working on a big goal, the feelings below are very common. If you're having trouble with any of these, scan the next few pages for reassurance.

MOTIVATE: Remove self-sabotage

(for feeling uninspired, discouraged, sad, hopeless)

1 Everything feels too hard and overwhelming.

Remember that tension seeks resolution.
Generate creative tension by comparing what you have now to how you want things to be. No need to make things seem better than they — or worse! Just take it one step at a time.

Challenges and effort must be balanced with sufficient recovery and rest.
Are you getting enough downtime away from your project?

2 Your goal doesn't excite you anymore.

Check for unwanted elements operating in the background.
Revisit the "If I knew I could have it" question on the Target Practice worksheet. Remove have-tos that don't fit. You get to choose what your unique dream looks like.

Assess whether your goal has changed.
As you experiment, encounter roadblocks and make progress, you'll likely have new insights about a desired outcome.

3 You keep trimming back your goal out of fear of failure.

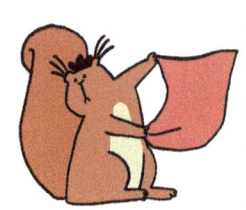

Obstacles are part of life and bring out our best.
Just like in fiction, challenges make the most of our abilities and create new opportunities. Constraints are a good thing.

Increase your bold ambition to fire up your imagination.
You may have compromised your original goal to ensure your chances of "reasonable" success. Try an I-Can-If question. "I can actually do: [seemingly impossible goal that benefits others] IF: [crazy, out of the box solution]."

CALM: Diffuse escapism

(for hiding out, feeling afraid, anxious, dread, overwhelmed)

1 You expect yourself to never, ever procrastinate or avoid tasks

See your "bad" habits as attempts at self-preservation.
Avoidance is a natural response to risk and danger, so treat your fears like a small, scared animal in a shoebox (kindly). Managing anxiety is an invaluable, lifelong skill that can be mastered.

You can't control the outcome, but you can improve the process.
Expect to cycle between feeling lost, then confident, then lost again. Decide to develop grit and perseverance and to navigate ambiguity.

2 You're paralyzed by catch-22 demands that ask the impossible.

You should know what you don't and be further along than you are.
We often don't realize we're doing this to ourselves, so shine a spotlight on the mental gymnastics. You can't have the wisdom without the experience.

You believe there's a way to dodge the cold buckets of water.
Accept it: some of your actions will fail. There are skills you need but don't have (and will later). Obstacles will arise that you won't see coming. Plus, this all happens amidst the struggles of regular life!

3 You're worried that you're secretly doomed.

Trust the heartfelt meaning behind your goal.
Use what you truly care about to rise above your fears. It takes gumption to make something from nothing. Your courage can inspire others to follow their own path and make the world a richer place.

The past does not predict the future.
Your unconscious expectations of failure are based on an older version of you. You've been wrong before, right? The future is not predetermined. You are always free to change and improve.

ACT: Get back on track when you drift

(for feeling unfocused, lost, confused, ineffective, unproductive)

1. You have no idea what to work on.

Tap back into your emotional connection to your goal.
Reread what you want, check in, then make your 3 best guesses for next steps. Just make them up as you go along.

Divide in half, then again and again.
Keep breaking down your larger goal into smaller parts until tasks start to feel familiar and doable. Simplify your goal to its bare bones benefit to others.

2. You have to figure out the exact right steps or you can't proceed.

You're rigidly following someone else's methods.
Success stories are always incomplete and deeply personal. There is no magic key with a guarantee that eliminates uncertainty. Catch yourself comparing, then shrug it off.

Acknowledge the abundance of your existing resources.
They're everywhere and include your varied fields of expertise and all your books, relationships, courses, and life experiences. Review just one and be inspired to experiment again.

3. You don't know how to translate a long-term goal into short-term demands.

Ask: what do I want and what actions will make that happen?
You'll be faced with two choices. Short-term demands that are likely unpleasant, but will help you reach your goal. Or distraction that relieves pressure. Which one do you want more? Just make a conscious choice.

Make sure to factor prep work into your timeline.
We often assume we're just going to jump straight into high-focus work, then panic and feel like we're behind when we don't. Build in time for planning and thinking too (different from escapist research).

GROW: Find childlike lessons for hard tasks

(for feeling powerless, small, inadequate, incompetent, untalented)

1. There's too much to do outside your comfort zone.

Find beginner's resources in children's curriculums and books.
Anything unknown can be learned. Map out your canyon of ignorance with broad categories where you'll need to acquire new skills. Be curious and enjoy the process!

It's okay if your approach is cobbled together.
We often can't see a method to our madness until after the fact. Who knows, you might even discover a new angle or unique blend of perspectives for others to build upon.

2. You can't bear to produce amateurish work, even temporarily.

Your fear of being imperfect is interfering with the learning process.
Allow yourself to produce utter garbage in the service of getting going. Imagine that you're building creative tenacity, just like a muscle.

Remind yourself of the failure stories of others.
NPR storyteller Ira Glass famously describes the gap between our taste and our abilities. Don't require mid- or professional-level skill from yourself as a student. Everyone has to start somewhere. You have nothing to prove.

3. You discount the power of tiny steps in the right direction.

Honor the power of baby steps.
Micromovements take from five seconds to five minutes to complete. "Clean out the garage" might mean you stand in the doorway and look around for one minute first. Success! What tiny steps could you take?

Practice robust simplicity for intimidating, complicated problems.
Now it's your turn to be the teacher. Even though it might feel silly, tell a child how to solve one of your thorniest problems with practical, achievable instructions.

ENERGIZE: Build confidence with brave honesty

(for feeling guilty, ashamed, jealous, embarrassed)

1. You're used to pumping yourself up to take action.

Don't rely on psyching yourself out to act.
This puts you at a disadvantage, because if you can't conjure up the energy, nothing happens. Pace yourself by dealing with reality and taking measured action.

Reject the hero or victim mindset.
It's the contrast between here and there that has all the energy to tap, not a role that you're playing. Ask how you can welcome your constraints to move away from learned helplessness.

2. You're fudging your data to avoid guilt and a lack of progress.

Be uncommonly brave about capturing neutral data.
There's no right or wrong way to do this, only a process that feels authentic and empowering, or hollow and fragile. You can choose to face unpleasant feelings and be honest at any time, even now.

It's no use being sneaky because you still know!
Pop the bubble of terror and shame (it's smaller than you think). The worst feeling is lying to yourself. Be your strongest, most reliable ally.

3. You keep stockpiling guilt and can't seem to make a fresh start.

Close your open loop of grievances against yourself.
Telling yourself the hard truth will help you embrace your human foibles and talents. Learn to fully acknowledge your struggles, forgive yourself and move on.

Don't chase someone else's life, be the only you there is.
Monitor your assumptions about other people's perfection. Never be willing to trade your life with another person because you will lose your hard-won talents and most valuable life lessons.

PHOTO BY FAUSTO GARCÍA-MENÉNDEZ

05
Resources

Further reading and staying in touch

> "If you limit your choice only to what seems possible or reasonable, you disconnect yourself from what you truly want, and all that's left is a compromise."
> - **Robert Fritz**, The Path of Least Resistance

I'm indebted to the work of Robert Fritz, which inspired me on this journey to put his ideas into practice.

Recommended books

The Path of Least Resistance, by Robert Fritz

A Beautiful Constraint, by Adam Morgan and Mark Barden

Thinking in Systems, by Donatella H. Meadows

A short course in creating what you always wanted to but couldn't before because nobody ever told you how because they didn't know either, by Robert Fritz

Grit, by Angela Duckworth

This Could Be Our Future, by Yancey Strickler

A Mind for Numbers, by Barbara Oakley

Bad Days in History, by Michael Farquhar

Staying in touch

Find accountability friends and connect with a community with these #hashtags:

#failforward #failforwardplanner #failforwardproject
#failforwardbuddy #failforwardfriend

Questions or comments? You'll find me at:
www.jennifernewcomb.com or www.letsfailforward.com.
+
Facebook: AuthorJenniferNewcomb
Twitter: Jennifer_NM
Pinterest: FailForwardPlanner
Instagram: LetsFailForward

About Jennifer

- I'm the author of two books on collaborative divorced family relationships and one on creativity.
- (The co-author of my first book, Carol Marine, is my kids' stepmom. We went from enemies to close friends while writing.)
- I've helped warring families end court battles and become parenting allies.
- I actually like public speaking, except for right before it happens.
- I've taught classes on writing, book proposals, blogging, web and graphic design, and filmmaking to kids and teens.
- I grew up in Madrid, Manila and all over the U.S.
- Now live in Eugene, Oregon, after a long stint in Austin.
- My husband and I are empty-nesters and between the two of us, we have five(!) daughters, two son-in-laws and one granddaughter.

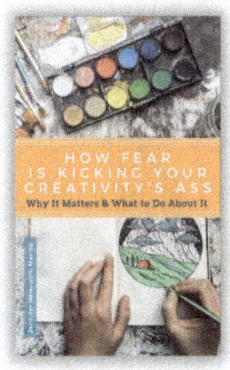  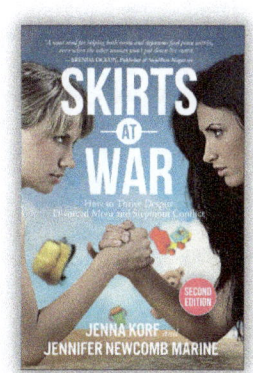

www.ingramcontent.com/pod-product-compliance
Lightning Source LLC
Chambersburg PA
CBHW082336300426
44109CB00045B/2381